MW01120818

life
can
be a
wild
ride

Saint Mary's Press
Christian Brothers Publications
Winona, Minnesota

life

can
be a

wild
ride

More Prayers
by Young Teens

Edited by Marilyn Kielbasa

Genuine recycled paper with 10% post-consumer waste.
Printed with soy-based ink.

The publishing team included Marilyn Kielbasa, development editor; Mary
Duerson, copy editor; James H. Gurley, production editor; Hollace Storkel,
typesetter; Cären Yang, designer; produced by the graphics division of Saint
Mary's Press.

Printed in the United States of America

Printing: 9 8 7 6 5 4 3 2 1

Year: 2008 07 06 05 04 03 02 01

ISBN 0-88489-484-3

Library of Congress Cataloging-in-Publication Data

Life can be a wild ride : more prayers by young teens / edited by Marilyn
Kielbasa.
     p. cm.
Includes index.
     ISBN 0-88489-484-3 (pbk. : alk. paper)
     1. Christian teenagers—Prayer-books and devotions—English.
I. Kielbasa, Marilyn.
     BV283.Y6 L54 2001
     242'.83—dc21
                                                 00-010069

Contents

Preface

Life Can Be a Wild Ride is the second collection of prayers by young teens published by Saint Mary's Press. The invitation for the first book of prayers, *Looking Past the Sky,* elicited over fourteen hundred submissions. The invitation for this second book resulted in over two thousand prayers from young teens in parishes and schools throughout North America.

Once again, the most difficult aspect of editing this book was choosing only about 10 percent of the prayers that were submitted. Thankfully, I had help from high school and college students who each read and rated about five hundred prayers. I made the final decisions based on their ratings while trying to achieve a balance between various factors: school and parish, boys and girls, themes, parts of the country, and so forth. Still, the opinions and comments of the young consultants was an invaluable starting point, and I am grateful to the following people for taking the time and energy to help out:

- Rob Brajkovich, Whiting, IN, Saint Mary's University
- Eli Bremer, Winona, MN, Saint Mary Parish
- Nat Bremer, Winona, MN, Saint Mary Parish
- Jaclyn Chentfant, Lackawanna, NY, Mount Mercy High School
- Nellie Gelhaus, Owen, WI, Saint Mary's University
- Jerome Graham, Hyattsville, MD, Saint Mary's University
- Ann Hansen, Spring Valley, MN, Saint Mary's University
- Jana Rozek, Winona, MN, Saint Mary's Parish
- Katie Stangler, Waseca, MN, Saint Mary's University

I regret that so many prayers had to be put in the "no" box. I am painfully aware that each prayer came from deep inside the heart of the young person who wrote it. If you are reading this and your prayer (or your student's prayer) is not among the 235 that were chosen for this book, please know that it is probably not because of the quality of the prayer. It may be because the prayer was one of the eight hundred prayers of thanksgiving that came in, or because it was the fourth really good prayer from your class or group. Fortunately, God doesn't have a "no" box. God hears and accepts *every* prayer from *every* person without giving a thought to balance, representation, word count, or page limits.

Like its predecessor, *Life Can Be a Wild Ride* is a collection of prayerful thoughts that run the gamut of human emotion and experience. It includes timeless reflections on painful losses, joyful celebrations, the struggles and gifts of relationships, questions about the future, the limitations of human understanding, and the day-to-day journey with God. The book also includes young teens' prayers about more timely topics as well: school violence, abortion, divorce, depression, and wartime atrocities are among the concerns that are voiced within these pages.

I am grateful to the teachers, catechists, DREs, youth ministers, and administrators who coordinated the efforts of their students and sent in their best efforts. Each day, you provide opportunities for young people to acknowledge and embrace their encounter with God. Your work is not easy, but it is quite clear that you make a big difference in the life of young people. Your efforts are applauded and appreciated. Thank you.

I am also grateful to each young person who wrote a prayer for *Life Can Be a Wild Ride,* whether or not it was sent in or selected for the book. You are God's work. You are making God's Reign a reality. You are a gift to the world. You are our cherished hope for the future. Thank you.

Marilyn Kielbasa
Editor

Part 1

God Is in the
Good Things

Oh, God, you have blessed me with more than I could ever find the words to thank you for. I appreciate the good health that you bring to my family and me day after day. I cherish the friendships that you give me the ability to nourish. I am grateful that you blessed me with two loving parents, and I love you for continually strengthening the bond between my sisters and me.

God, you help me time and again through the pain and strife in my life. And regardless of the wrongdoing I may render, you stand by me through it all. I worship you with all my heart and soul, and I'll forever keep my faith in you. Amen.

Angela Donizetti
Holy Family School, Norwood, NJ

Dear God,
I thank you for blessing me with such a glorious and fulfilling life with loving parents. I thank you for my wonderful personality and charm.

Meagan M. Rodkey
Saint Luke Parish, Carol Stream, IL

If I could **count all the stars** in the sky, **multiply them by infinity,** and then **add one,** the number still wouldn't compare to how much you love and care for the world. Thank you, God, for everything you have given me and all that I will receive from you in the future. I especially thank you for your everlasting love and kindness.

Jessica K. Flanagan
Saint Mary Parish, Durand, IL

Lord, thank you for this **marvelous morning.**
　　Bless the birds that go soaring.
　　Help the day not to be boring.

Lord, thank you for this **wonderful day.**
　　Help me to follow your way.
　　Listen to me when I pray.

Lord, thank you for this **beautiful night.**
　　Bless me with all your might.
　　Help me remove all my fright.

Eighth grade religious education class
Saint Benedict Parish, Duluth, GA

Dear Daddy,
Thank you for the past, the present, and the future. Thank you for the sunrise. It's like your smile greeting me with a chance to start all over. Thank you for the sunset. It lets me know I can start again tomorrow, learning from my mistakes.

　　Thanks for parents who have "been there done that," and who, from their experiences, try to keep me from harm. (Okay, I'm not always grateful, but please help me to be.) Thanks for words, that they may be used to glorify your name. Thanks for giving me special gifts, that I may give them back to you.

　　I love you Daddy! You're my first love, my best friend, and my favorite teacher.
　　Your precious child,
　　Deanna

Deanna M. Jones
Saint Ann School, Bartlett, TN

Thank you, God, for this day.

Thank you for protecting me and letting me live for another day.

Lord, my life is for you.

Amen.

Heidi Alexandra Fontenot
Saint Patrick Parish, Baton Rouge, LA

God,
Aloha again from me, Michelle Ciesielski.
I just wanted to say thank you.
Thank you for me.
Every bit of me. Not just bits and pieces.
Thanks for the good, the bad, and the ugly.
Thanks for my New York accent, my big cheek bones, and the
way I play basketball (even though I stink at it).
Thanks for my sense of humor; without it I don't know what I
would do.
Thanks for the way I talk to people.
Thanks so much for my writing ability. Sometimes I think it is
the only talent I have (even though I know it isn't).
Thanks for my no-sing voice and the way I handle public
embarrassment.
Thank you for my last name that no one can spell or
pronounce except my close friends.
Thank you for my beliefs molded from the lessons I have
learned.
Thank you for me.
All of me. Michelle Ciesielski.
The girl who has little dilemmas, but no crisis except for her
messy room.
Thanks so much.

Michelle Ciesielski
Saint Agnes Cathedral Parish, Springfield, MO

God in heaven,
Thank you for my eyes,
    so I can see this glorious world you've created.
For my nose,
    so I can smell the flowers you planted on that creation day.
For my mouth,
    so I can stand up for what I believe in.
For my ears,
    so I can hear the sweet singing of the birds in the early
        morn.
For my hands,
    so I can do work for myself.
For my feet,
    so I can carry myself from one place to the next.
For the love that you show me,
    so I may feel wanted.
For my heart,
    so I may love others the way you love me.
For my life,
    so I can live every day to please and serve others.
Amen.

Ashley M. Rachubinski
Seton Catholic Middle School, Menasha, WI

Dear God,

Thank you for everything you have given me.

 Please help me **to do good in life,**

and help me to be the best I can be. Amen.

Erica Johnson
Saint Mary Parish, Kalamazoo, MI

God, I'm calling upon you to tell you thanks. You helped me through a hard time in my life, and because of you I now have a smile on my face every day.

> I have new friends that help me when I'm down.
> I have no reason to be mad.
> I know you love me, and so do a lot of others.
> I know I'll never feel the way I did again
> with you by my side.

Thanks again. I love you.

Brandi Wildhaber
Immaculate Conception School, Jefferson City, MO

God, thank you **very, very, very** much for anything

and everything you have ever done for me.

Nicholas Mangione
Saint Nicholas Ukrainian Catholic Church, Watervliet, NY

I am thankful for technology that helps us do things right,
That makes our lives easy, and fills our homes with light.
I am thankful for the weather, that spreads beauty all around,
That causes leaves to grow on trees, and snow to fall to the
        ground.
I am thankful for my family and friends, who fill my life with
        love.
I am thankful for my God, who watches me from above.
I am thankful for the moon, the stars, the sun, the sky, the shade.
But Jesus, most of all I'm thankful for the sacrifice you made.

Nicholas V. Romeo
Saint Clement Mary Hofbauer School, Baltimore, MD

Thank you, O God, for all that you have given us.
We are grateful, though sometimes we fuss.
Thank you for the earth, the land, and the sea.
But most of all, God, thank you for me.
Thanks for our families who help us when we're feeling sad.
Thanks for our friends who comfort us in the midst of bad.
Thank you for the special talents that we can share.
But most importantly, thank you for letting us love and care.
And even after thanking you a million times,
Somehow, it is just not enough.

Jessica DellaRose
Our Lady of Hope/Saint Luke School, Baltimore, MD

God,
You are always there for me when I need you.
For that, *I thank you.*
You have always listened to me. For that, *I thank you.*
You have always watched over me. For that, *I thank you.*
You have created me and watch me grow.
For life, I thank you.

Marianne Delehanty
Holy Family School, Norwood, NJ

Dear God,
I know that Jesus spent his life giving and giving and never
asked for anything in return. God, you have given me so many
things that I often forget to thank you. Please help me to notice
and to use the gifts and talents you gave me correctly, and not
take them for granted.

Isolt Garcia
Saint Clare of Montefalco School, Chicago, IL

Thank you, God, for this day.

The events that occurred are long gone away.

Yet **the memory stays,** and **I hold it tight**
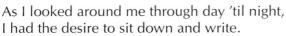

As I drift asleep into the quiet night.

Jennifer L. Kernan
Saint Denis/Saint Columba School, Hopewell Junction, NY

As I looked around me through day 'til night,
I had the desire to sit down and write.
The world seemed hopeless and the people, unclear.
So I uncovered these things which were veiled in despair and
　　　fear.
I felt the sun's glowing warmth. I saw the sea-sparkling blue.
I heard the heavens' whispering winds, and then I thought of
　　　you.
I remembered all those days, and how you held me close.
When I was feeling so far down were the times you cared the
　　　most.
It took me quite a while, God, to realize you are truly by me.
But now I want to thank you for your patience when my faith
　　　was oh so blurry.
Dear God, I want to thank you for my loving family and friends,
Who have sheltered me through everything, always there 'til
　　　the very end.
God, I'd like to thank you for my favorite gift of all.
It's the gift of love you've blessed me with that overwhelms me
　　　at the slightest call.
Thank you for your wonders, and thank you, God, for you,
For I have learned your love is always,
And I thank you, I truly do.

Chelsea Wisdom
Saint Paschal Baylon School, Thousand Oaks, CA

Thank you, God, for life.
But why is there cancer and disease that can take life away?
Thank you, God, for family.
But why are some children orphans?
Thank you, God, for strength.
But why are there children who never have a chance to walk?
Thank you, God, for a house and food.
But why are some people homeless and hungry?
Thank you, God, for your love.
Everyone has that.

Caitlin Joosten
Saint Vincent de Paul School, Wisconsin Rapids, WI

Dear God,
Thank you for the glowing moon, and for the bandit raccoon.
Thank you for the colorful trees, and for the yellow bees.
Thank you for the green grass, and for the slippery bass.
Thank you for the twinkling stars, and for the swirly planet of
            Mars.
Thank you for the glistening lakes, and for the gobbling jakes.
Thank you for the different rocks, and for the sly red fox.
Thank you for the shimmering sun, and for all the wonderful fun.

Owen Gellings
Saint Matthew School, Campbellsport, WI

Lord God, thank you for *love* within our hearts.

Lord God, thank you for *gifts* within our hands.

But most of all, Lord God, thank you for *life* within our souls.

Kevin D'Amico
Saint Charles Parish, Boardman, OH

17

Thank you for the *a*nimals that are rare.

Thank you for the *b*eauty of everything out there.

Thank you for the *c*olors of fall and the *d*ecisions of all.

Thank you for the *e*arth from beginning to end.

Thank you for my *f*amily and my very special friend.

Thank you for the *g*rass and the *h*ope of my class.

Thank you for the *i*slands and the weed and the *j*unk we don't
        need.

Thanks for the *k*ids of the future.

Thank you for the *l*ife from a culture.

Thank you for the *m*aple trees and their bark.

Thank you for *N*oah and his ark.

Thank you for *O*ceans though not near for all

and especially for *p*igs in the stall.

Thank you for the *q*uiet from others.

Thanks for *r*espect from our sisters and brothers.

Thank you for the *S*hapes, the sky, and clouds that are white.

Thank you for the *t*alents that are right.

Thanks for the *U*niverse that's ours.

Thanks for the *V*ines that climb for hours.

Thank you for the *W*atermelons that are fat and thin,

and thank you for *X*anthein.

Most of all thank you for *y*our unconditional love that's the
        best,

And for our *Z*eal and *Z*est!

Amanda Knapp
Holy Family Junior High School, Elmira, NY

Thank you, God, for the grass and the trees; thank you for the
    cool summer breeze.
Thank you, God, for my mom and dad; thank you for the cat I
    had.
Thank you, God, for the clouds in the sky; thank you for my
    Grandma's peach pie.
Thank you, God, for my fat, little dog; thank you for the cows
    and the hogs.
Thank you, God, for my educated teachers; thank you for my
    very smart preacher.
Thank you, God, for the clothes on my back; thank you for my
    shoes that are black.
Thank you, God, for my guardian angel's wings; thank you for
    everything.

Hanna Radel
Saint Michael Parish, Kingsley, IA

Thank you, God, for the little things
    that often come our way.
The things that we take for granted,
Don't remember to say when we pray—
    the unexpected courtesy,
    the special, kindly deeds,
A helping hand reached out to us
    at a time we are in need.
Oh, make us aware, dear God,
    of small daily graces
That come to us with joyful surprises
From never-dreamed-of places.

Brittany Carlon
Saint Charles School, Boardman, OH

Thank you, God, for letting me see your glory through nature. I see you in the majesty of the mountains. I feel your warmth and love in the rays of the sun. I see you in the sunset reflected on the waters of the ocean. I feel your spirit when the wind blows my hair into my face, and I thank you. I see you through all of your people. I see them laughing, playing, jumping, and crying. Through your good people I learn what you expect of me and learn to be good myself. Thank you, oh God, for the great many gifts you have given me. You have blessed me, and I am truly thankful. Amen.

Alisan Follingstad
Saint Thomas More School, Kansas City, MO

Gratitude fills my spirit.
My God cares for me like a flower in a garden.
God is my armor in a battle that keeps me safe.
My great protector, thank you!
Glory to Yahweh, the generous one.

I cannot stop singing songs of praise and thanks.
God surrounds me with people,
who wrap me in their love.
My God is always near,
like the warm sun on a summer day.
The Great One comes to my aid with wisdom.
Glory to Yahweh, the generous one.

My heart is overflowing,
I fall to my knees.
Sheltering Father, my life is in your hands.
You shower me with your gifts,
and I praise your greatness.
Glory to Yahweh, the generous one.

Erin Grady
Saint Norbert School, Paoli, PA

Dear God,

I look at myself today, and I see how you made me.

You didn't make me the most self-controlled.

You didn't make me the smartest.

You didn't make me the best at sports.

You didn't make me the kindest.

You didn't make me famous.

You didn't make my ideas stop being the lamest.

But you made me, ME, and for that I thank you, God. Because I don't want to be anyone else but who I am. Amen.

Teresa Prince
Saint Robert Bellarmine School, Omaha, NE

Thank you for the sun, and the rain.
Thank you for the stars at night, and the snow in the winter.
Thank you for letting me have so many good days, and helping me through the bad days.
Thank you for teachers, who help me to be all I can, and thank you for those people who make my life challenging.
Thank you for my friends and family, and flowers.
Jesus, please help me to help those in need. Help me to be strong and to choose the better choice in life.
Please help me to love, even when I find it hard to.
Thank you for so many good things.
Thank you for giving me life.
Amen.

Jody Allsbrook
Mount Saint Joseph Academy, Buffalo, NY

I **love** to go outside and enjoy the green, beautiful trees and grass that you made. I **love** it when the leaves change colors to their brilliant reds, oranges, and browns. I **love** to rake all of the leaves up and jump in them.

Out of all the creatures and things you have ever made, I want you to know that I **love** my family. I **love** how they take care of me when I am sick. I **love** how they get so excited for me when I hit a home run or make a basket. I **love** how they comfort me when I am sad. God, thank you for everything!

Toni Osborne
Holy Spirit Parish, Indianapolis, IN

Thank you for raindrops on spider webs,
    peanut butter and jelly sandwiches,
    nightlights,
    and the giggle of a two-year-old.
Thank you for bedtime stories
    and rainbows, too.
Thank you for a kitten's whiskers,
    a puppy's attempted growl,
    and the coffee that keeps our parents going.
Thank you for basketball,
    and every other little thing that makes the world go round.
Amen.

Lindsey Tarbox
Saint Ann School, Bartlett, TN

I thank you for the eyes I see with.
      Without them I would be blind to your greatness.
I thank you for the ears I hear with.
      Without them I would be deaf and not hear your praises.
I thank you for the lips I speak with.
      Without them I wouldn't be able to speak your prayers.
I thank you for my family.
      Without them I would be lonely.
I thank you for the house I live in.
      Without it I would be cold.
I thank you for the food I eat.
      Without it I would go hungry.
Most of all, I thank you for my life.
      Without it I would not be alive in your presence.

Megan Clarke
Holy Spirit Parish, Sioux Falls, SD

God, thank you for our butter
And thank you for our bread.
We thank you for the pillow
On which we rest our head.
We thank you for the universe,
The living, and the dead,
Yes, *all the world thanks you,* God.

We thank you for the sun and clouds,
We thank you for the rain.
We thank you for our siblings,
Who sometimes are a pain.
For everything we have in life,
We thank you in your name.
Yes, *all the world thanks you,* God.

Dylan Lamb
Annunciation School, Minneapolis, MN

God,
You gave me eyes to see your miracles and lips to sing your
praise.
You gave me legs so I can dance and hands to do your work.
You gave me feet to walk in faith and a mind so I can pray.
You gave me ears to hear your voice and happiness to spread.
You gave me arms to help the poor and a heart to love the world.
You gave me everything I have, from my head down to my toes.
Without you I would be alone, afraid and meek and weak.
But having you in my life gives me hope to go on.
Thank you, God.

Samantha Reed
Nativity School, Dubuque, IA

Thank you, God, for creating us,
    For giving us life,
    For showing us your love.
Thank you for protecting us.

Thank you, God, for all of us in our class:
    Brian, Courtney, Sean, and Melanie.
Thank you for our families,
    the moon and the stars,
    flowers,
    the Internet,
    and chocolate cookies.
Help us to do your will and be the best we can be.

Help us to be **best friends with you, God.** Amen.

Special needs religious education class
Saint Benedict Parish, Duluth, GA

Thank you, God, for what you've let me accomplish in life. You've given me so much, and most of it I really don't deserve. I have a loving family and a house filled with warmth. I have great friends, an excellent education, and much more. Many people are so unfortunate, and you have made me just opposite. Thank you, God, for the talents and gifts you have filled me with. Thank you, God, for what you've given me to make my life so beautiful!

Lindsay Jo Bruns
Saint Boniface Parish, Garner, IA

Part 2

God Is in the Changes

God, I know my life is in your hands.
Life is hard, God, but you somehow always give me hope.
The hope you give makes me stronger.
In your hands, God, I am happy.
I feel safe when you are near.
You carry me to my destinations.
You guide me.
Without you, God, I am lost.
You are constantly there to pick me up.
When I am happy, you are happy with me.
When I am sad, you support me.
Life is always changing.
No matter what comes, good or bad, you are there for me.
You are my path to follow.
You lead me.
I thank you!
God, I know my life is in your hands.

Allison Tokolish
Saint Rose of Lima School, Haddon Heights, NJ

Hi, God, it's me, Andrew. I have been thinking. Lately, I haven't taken you seriously. I haven't been honest. I have tried to hide some things too. I have even questioned you about me, even though I know it is wrong. **God, bring me back.** I really need you. Growing up is hard!

Andrew
Saint Joseph School, Cottleville, MO

I am gift.

God made me who I am, so I am gift.
No matter what others say, God loves me for me,
Not for what others want me to be.
I am who I am,
Nothing more, nothing less.
I am my own person.
I am special.

I am gift!

Leonard A. Billé
Saint Bernadette School, Brooklyn, NY

Dear God,
We hear warnings to stay away from drugs; but when the
    pressure becomes too much, do you expect us to turn
    and walk away?

Sometimes I need help.

When a friend wants to stay out that extra ten minutes when
    you know you can't, what do you do?

Sometimes I need help.

When your mom asks you if your homework is done and you
    want to go out and play, I don't know what to do.

Sometimes I need help.

When I get picked on for something and want to fight, it's hard
    to know what to do.

Sometimes I need help.

It's scary to think what I would do without you. If it weren't for
    your guidance, I would never make it through the day.
    That's why if you ever see me in a tough situation, I
    would like to know that I can trust in you to guide me
    the right way, and not let me make a bad decision.
    Just remember, God,

Sometimes I need help.

Matt Czerkowicz
Mount Saint Charles Academy, Woonsocket, RI

Bottled up inside,
are the words I've never said, God,
the feelings I deeply hide,
inside my wondering head.
I know you can read me inside and out, God,
I know that without a simple doubt in my mind.
You can see it in my eyes,
read it on my face.
Trapped inside are the conscious torturing lies of the past
that I cannot replace.
No more wishing for the past; it wasn't meant to be.
It didn't seem to nearly last.
So I have to set myself free, God.
Teenage thoughts rip me apart inside and out.
Please, God, help me through these teenage years.
Amen.

Jaclyn
Saint Benedict School, Holmdel, NJ

Dear God,
When I wake up the day is new
and full of many things to do.
Basketball, tennis, and soccer
plus homework that fills up my locker.
Although my life is busy
and sometimes drives me into a tizzy,
I thank you for all the fun things I do.
But I ask for the strength to guide me through.

Karrie Hagedorn
Blanchet School, Salem, OR

A teen is emotional and fun to be around.
A teen is love.
A teen is like the brave wind; a teen is smart and always
      changing.
A teen is love.
A teen is rebellious, creative, and playful.
A teen is love.
God, I am asking you to protect all the teens in this world,
      including myself. Guide us in our development and
      forgive us for our sins. Protect us against all evils.
      Give us the strength and the wisdom to always make
      the right choices and to always do good for others,
      because . . .
a teen is love.
A teen is the future of this world, the hope for generations to
      come.
A teen is love.

Klaus Peter Kruger
Holy Rosary School, Antioch, CA

God,
Help me in my days and nights,
When I'm mad, and in big fights,
Help all kids, with their grades and school,
Help me follow all your rules,
Help me with my friends all day,
Don't let me desert them, or call them mean names,
Most of all, teach me to **PRAY,** to **LOVE,** and to **SERVE,**
In your Son's way.

Eric Wiltz
Epiphany School, Miami, FL

Dear God,
Help me to discover who I really am. Help me to find the lost soul dwelling beneath the shields, the masks, the fake smiles. Help me to rid myself of these disguises, to overcome the ever-present feeling of loneliness. Help me to discover my individuality and my ability to be accepted. Help me to understand who I should be, and what my purpose in life is. For then, and only then, will the true me be shining through. And I know this because, when I find myself, I'll be among the stars. Amen.

Ashley Coyle
Holy Rosary School, Claymont, DE

God, you probably already know I had a bad day. I got teased about being short, and some of my friends accused me of doing some things I didn't do. I got a C and an F on my two tests. So maybe tomorrow you could tell them to accept me for who I am and help me to gain confidence in myself to do better in my schoolwork. But right now I want to thank you for all I have and bless the people who are less fortunate than me. Amen.

Adam Reed Fitch
Sacred Heart School, Coshocton, OH

Dear God,

I need your help. I have a decision to make. I have **no clue** what to do. Can you help me make the right decision? Please help me to make the right choice.

Lauren
Most Precious Blood Parish, Hazleton, PA

Dear God,
Help me remember before every game that **nothing on earth**
shall be cherished more than you. I want to perform
to my capability, but above all I want to have fun. Let me
practice good sportsmanship, and help me to remember
that it is just a game. Amen.

Dane Hughes
Immaculate Conception School, Jefferson City, MO

Help me, God, not to be pressured by my friends
And by others who I meet.
I don't want to bring my life to an end
By an act of conformity.

Help me, God, to face my fears
And to stand up for what I believe.
I wish to live successfully for all my years
And earn all I receive.

Help me, God, to tame my anger
When I'm filled with steam.
Violence just causes more danger
As little as it seems.

Help me, God, to make good decisions
In all my years as a teen.
I know there may be some collisions
As I try to follow my dreams.

Thank you, God, for always being there
When I was always in need.
I know your love is everywhere
As well as your great deeds.

Matthew Dimalanta Camorongan
Holy Rosary School, Antioch, CA

Dear God, I pray for someone I can talk to. Someone I know will not tell my secrets. Someone who enjoys my company. **Someone like me.** Someone who I can open up to and who will open up to me. Someone who knows what I am going through, and can be there for me.

Dear God, I hope I am not asking for too much, but please try to help me find that **certain someone.**

Sarah Ramos
Mount Saint Charles Academy, Woonsocket, RI

Jesus, I have a problem I just can't face.
Every day I go through disgrace.
Please help me go through this day,
Without criticizing others or telling them to go away.
At school I am cruel to those who do nothing to me.
Please help me, Lord Jesus. Please answer me.
Why can't I be kind to others who need me?
All I do is tease them, and I know it hurts them inside.
When I am disrespectful, it makes me just want to run and hide.
I try to act cool, but it doesn't work.
It just makes people feel put down and hurt.
I am not that kind of person.
Please let me see the sweet little girl that I used to be.
Please help me be me and not someone who hurts people that
     I see.
Please, Lord Jesus, please help me be the kind, generous person
     I used to be. Amen.

Ashley Youngkrantz
Saint Christopher School, Vandalia, OH

God, love me for who I am.
Love me for the person I hide inside,
The person that won't come out,
Not for the person that I act.
For that person is not me,
Just hiding the real me.
The real me is stuck somewhere in my heart,
The me I am afraid to show.
Help me stand up for what I believe,
No matter what other people say.
If I hide myself now,
I will be hiding the real me, forever.
I praise you, God, for your strength and
Your guidance.
For when I speak to you,
I speak from the real me in my heart.
Amen.

Carina Ann Vitullo
Saint Charles School, Boardman, OH

Dear God,
I see so many teens today who have gone
their own way without you. Their lives are

SO EMPTY.

They are calling out for your help. Please send
your Holy Spirit to show them your way.
Guide them to people who care and will
help them. Please help them to see the goodness
in life that comes from you. Amen.

Katie Turnbull
Saint Dominic Parish, Sigel, PA

Oh, God, please help me for I know what is to come.
With so many dangers and so many fears, what will I become?
There will be times when I'm depressed; there will be times
  when I'm under pressure.
With so many different choices, how can I be sure?
I will be pressured to do so much, like drugs, gangs, and
  violence.
I know I'll be so scared, God, so please give me some good
  sense.
There will be times when I make bad choices; there will be
  times when I make mistakes.
Please help me get through those times, no matter how much it
  takes.
I know I've already asked so much, but I have one more request:
  Please help me try my hardest, and always do my best.

Kristen DelMonaco
Saint Maria Goretti School, Schiller Park, IL

Dear God,
The pressure's rising. I don't know what to do.
In my time of confusion, I turn to you.
You give me strength, God, in my time of need.
You answer me, God, whenever I plead.
When I ask for forgiveness, you grant me love.
It's the eternal forgiveness that comes from above.
When you are around me, all I feel is peace.
The harmony and love shall never cease.
I need you now. I need you here.
But I don't need to worry, for you are always near.
I love you, God, with all my heart.
And I'll always know, we'll never part.

Amanda Wallich
Saint Roman School, Milwaukee, WI

Dear God,

Right now in my life I have been coming up with

VERY BIG QUESTIONS, and I need some ANSWERS.

Please help me in finding the answers to my questions. Amen.

Andrew Aten
Church of the Incarnation, Centerville, OH

Dear God,
You have put me on this earth for a reason.
And yet I know not what it is.
When will I know?
When will I find out?

Will I ever know?

I do not understand right now.
But I know you are here to lead me, so **I place my faith in you.**

Caitlin Alvarez
Saint Catherine of Siena School, Metairie, LA

Dear God,
I'm growing up now, and nothing is the same.
Now that I'm changing, life means more to me than just a game.
I pray to you, and I know you'll be there for all the good and
        bad times that we share.
I know I'm not perfect, but I'm trying my best.
Please, God, help me pass this difficult life test.
I'll try my hardest, for as long as I live,
And give everyone all I can give.
Amen.

Wendy Chatelain
Saint Mark School, Chalmette, LA

O God, please strengthen all kids who are teased and made fun of. Let them know they are **stronger** in character, and **braver** in spirit than the teaser. Let them grow in love, and never let them wander from your holy church. Amen.

Nick Nudo
Sacred Heart School, Conroe, TX

God, help me to be patient with my friends, family,

and everyone I come in contact with.

Help me to be *more understanding* when things

don't go the way I want them to. Amen.

Colleen Furniss
Saint Paul Parish, Oswego, NY

Dear God,
People make fun of me at school. I know I'm different, but that's okay, because I believe in myself. I know they are afraid of my strengths. That is why they make fun of me.
    I don't follow the crowd.
    I don't wear fashionable clothes.
    I don't wear stylish shoes.
    I don't care about the latest trends.
    I care about something else. I care about you, God.
For that I praise you. Amen.

Matt Reardon
Saint Hedwig School, Wilmington, DE

Going home that autumn day
Walking on my way
I saw a girl just sitting there
Looking in the air.

As I walked by she started to cry.
I thought my oh my.
I decided to sit right next to her.
All I could see was her face, a blur.

As I was talking
She got up and started walking.
I cried out, "Wait," but it was too late.
She started to run.
That's when it all had begun.

I started to run after her.
I called out, "Wait!" and she said, "Sure."
As she turned around to my surprise
The school's outcast was before my eyes.

Her name is Sanda.
At school she's called the big fat Panda.
I would be her friend, but
She's so out of trend.

My next step forward was my biggest step to take.
The outcast is before me. Am I the fake?
I tried to run, I tried to hide, but
I couldn't get away from my own pride.

I sat down as we both cried,
Friends forever side by side.

Caitlyn Peatee
Gesu School, Toledo, OH

Dear God,
You are always glad to listen to all my prayers, no matter what I ask. I know I ask a lot of you, but for once I'm not asking for an A on a test or to win a game. I'm in need of your guidance.

I have a very good friend that I have known all my life. We have always lived in different places, yet we have always been close. Lately we have grown our different ways, which is sad because the calls are very few. As if school, sports, and boys have become more important to us than each other. God, I'm in need of your love and guidance to show us the way back to each other. Amen.

Sarah Grassman
Blanchet School, Salem, OR

Dear God,

Work is hard. I know what has to be done, but I don't feel like doing it. So, I ask you for help. God, give me the **ambition** and **strength** to do what I must, even if it is hard or tiresome. I thank you, O God.

Mike Beres
Saint Mary Catholic Community, Crown Point, IN

Dear God,
Please forgive me for saying bad stuff in school and for getting angry at home. It's just that I get so ticked, and I cannot hold it inside any longer. So please forgive me. Amen.

Aaron J. Barnard
Saint Joseph Parish, Good Thunder, MN

Oh, great God up in heaven,
Sitting on a throne above,
I offer you my life, my day,
But most of all my love.
Today in school, oh, God, I pray,
Help me to be kind
To those not as well liked as me,
And to keep your Son in mind.
Try to keep the kids from mocking me,
Protect me from bitter words,
Don't let me make a fool of myself,
This I ask, oh, God.
I know, that even though I try,
Not all the things I do
Will turn out as well as I wish,
For that is the will of you.
Dear God, protect me from sin and lies,
Let me have a little fun.
I'll try to keep from swearing,
And I'll only play when my work is done.
God, I know that you cannot grant
All of these wishes I make,
Just help me obey my mom and dad,
And the commandments I'll try not to break.
I can only do this with your help,
Please help me because I am told,
That if I can do all of these things,
I will know you until I am old.

Nicole Vitale
Saint Thomas à Becket Parish, Jefferson Hills, PA

Dear God,

Life can be so **difficult.** Everything seems to change. Sometimes I wonder if I can make it through the day. I look beyond the clouds and wonder what it holds. Life must be easier somewhere else. Then I think of what God gave me, and I know that some people have a harder life than I do.

Life can be so *easy.* There are times when things go smoothly and your way. You're floating on cloud nine.

Life is too *short.* We can't get all we want done. There is too much left to discover and hold; so much to see and hear.

Life is too *long.* We see too much crime and death. We know too much wrong.

Life is *love.* I love my life and my Lord. God lovingly gave us life, so life we should love. We should love our enemies and one another.

Life doesn't make sense in teenage years, but God still loves each life.

Rachel
Nativity of Our Lord School, Orchard Park, NY

Oh, God, please guide us through rough times.
Calm our fears.
Abolish our doubt.
Let us see the unseen,
hear the unheard,
and feel the forgotten.
Let us accept all people, no matter their race or religion.
Please give us someone we can confide in, someone with whom
          we can share our problems, our hopes, and our secrets.

Scott Kennedy
Saint Mary Parish, Franklin, OH

Please help me, dear God!
Oh, I'm so blue, I'm having a terrible day.
    My parents are crabby.
    I'm a mess.
    I have no friends,
    I'm failing tests.
Please have mercy, God.
I need to be blessed!
Help me through my life,
without me being a pest.
I'm down to the last string,
being tempted to death,
packed with activities,
I'm definitely not bored.
Give me a REST!

Oh, how I love you and all you do,
Oh, how I love you.
Please help me through my mixed-up teenage years.
Please,
        help
            me,
                dear
                    God!
                        Amen.

Justine Beckman
Saint Boniface School, Elgin, NE

Dear God,
I pray that tomorrow will be a great day. I also pray that the
upcoming tests are not really bad. When I get the test, please
help me not to forget what I study.

Jessica Stolt
Saint John the Baptist Parish, Minnesota Lake, MN

Dear God,

Every day I am faced with small choices that are easily

resolved, but sometimes I come across big decisions that

can be scary. If I jump in, what will happen? Will I start with

confidence, but trip and fall? Will I make the right choice?

I don't know, but I believe that you will help me choose wisely.

So, God, the next time I am faced with a decision too big for

me alone, I'll smile an inner smile, and *JUMP* **into your arms.**

Sophie DiLoreto
Saint Catherine of Siena School, Metairie, LA

God, I'm confused about some things.
Like growing up.
It's hard to be the person I'm meant to be.
Sometimes I do things just to fit in.
Not because I want to.
And when I mess up, it's very embarrassing.
Sometimes I'm depressed for no reason at all.
And sometimes I couldn't be happier.
Sometimes I feel lonely, even though I know I have friends.
I'm more sensitive now than before.
I don't know . . .
I could just use some help, God.
If you could guide me through this,
That would be awesome.
I love you.

Stephanie
Saint Thomas Aquinas School, Derry, NH

Dear God,

As a teenager I am thinking about deeper things than I used to, like my future and my goals. I seem to be more responsible most of the time. And much more is expected of me. Please, help me have the courage and the will to do what is right. Help me choose the right goals for my future. These decisions will affect me for a long time, maybe the rest of my life. Also, I ask to become closer to you in faith and love. If I sometimes doubt or offend you, I am sorry. As you forgive me, God, help me forgive others, even when it is hard to do. For without you I am lost. I love you, God. Amen.

Drew Nemec
Saint Clare of Assisi School, Ellisville, MO

I am the painting that God paints.
I am a pack of pink pastels.
I am the wind on a crisp fall day.
I am the snow in mid-December.
I am a fork in the road.
I am a path that leads to home.
I am a marshmallow in hot chocolate.
I am a glass of ice-cold lemonade.
I am watermelon on a hot summer day.
I am the song of the hummingbird.
I am a mountain from which the eagle soars.
I am the friend she never had.
I am the teacher from which you will learn.
I am the curls upon your head.
I am the smile that never goes away.
I am the secret of the black widow.
I am the butterfly caught in her web.
I am the shoulder on which to cry.
I am the child wondering why.
I am me—*a gift to be given.*

Stephanie Fairbanks
Saint John the Baptist Parish, Tipp City, OH

Dear God, you are so loving and forgiving. Thank you for making the beautiful earth, and especially for making me. If I have failed you in any way, I am very sorry. I will try to be more like Jesus. At times, it's very hard, but I will strive to make a difference.

Please help me in my hard times, because I can't always handle it. Grant me the gift of courage. When I want to stand up for the right thing, I get too nervous. It happens to me when I take tests, too. I get nervous, and I can't even read the questions right. My parents and everyone else just think I need to study more. You're the only one who understands. Thank you, God.

James Held
Saint John School, Westminster, MD

Dear God, please bless us during our game
and help us to play to the best of our ability.
May neither team have injuries and keep all the players safe.
"May they walk and not grow weary; may they
run and not grow faint."
May the best team win and honor you in your glory.

Pat McCann
Holy Spirit Parish, Sioux Falls, SD

Dear God,
You created me, and I am your work in progress. Help me to listen to what people have to say. Help me learn to talk things out with my family and friends. Let me be more truthful. Teach me to be kind to all people in life. Amen.

Stephanie Shindledecker
Our Lady of Hope/Saint Luke School, Baltimore, MD

God, I need you to help me during my quarrels
And to help me with my lack of morals.
Please be with me through the day.
There's really nothing else I can say.
My parents are really nice.
My friends I really can't say the same.
I have two real friends,
But I guess it's myself to blame.
The girls make fun of me because I play with children's toys,
And then it gets around to the boys.
Do you think I have a chance?
It's my personal life I have to enhance.
Tell me, God, I need to know.
God, I admire you dearly, and I love you too.
But still a sign you do not show.
God, I need you!

Lori Anne Hart
Sacred Heart School, West Reading, PA

God, **what's wrong with me?** Sometimes I love church and everything that goes along with it, and sometimes I have no clue what it's for. I keep getting told that you love me no matter what, but sometimes I kind of feel that I'm getting farther away from you because I sin, and I know it's my fault. But I really need your help to find you in my life. And thank you so much for helping me play volleyball so well.

I play for God. I love you.

Ida Clay
Sacred Heart School, Conroe, TX

I am just like a leaf—growing on God's green earth.

I **grow** and **grow** until I can **grow** no more.

Then I become aged and fall from the tree.

As I fall, I think of what a wonderful life I had.

Soon I'll be in heaven with God.

Nate Goedde
Saint Michael Parish, Kalida, OH

God, at my age now,
I find it hard somehow
To want to listen to what you say.
You seem so big and so far away.

Your power just overwhelms me.
Should I be afraid? Just let me be!
But I know you are persistent
And care enough to send the very best.

Just like instant messaging,
You always keep in touch.
That's why I honestly admit
That I love you very much.

Benjamin Adamski
Saint Stanislaus Kostka Parish, Bay City, MI

Part 3

God Is in the
People We Love

To my family, great and small, we are the best family of them all. Even though we go through tough times, it doesn't mean we don't have any time to get together and talk. I love to sit and talk to you, especially when we are all together. And the last thing I want to say may be small but that's okay. They are only three words, but they mean the most to me—I love you! And I hope you love me the same way. Amen.

Adam Farrell
Saint Dominic Parish, Sigel, PA

Dear God,
Why did my parents get a divorce? I guess they weren't meant to be. Was it me? Who was it? I see all these other kids whose parents are not divorced. Why did it have to happen to my family? I hope that when I get married someday, I will be one of those people who don't get divorced. Please help my family and me and all those who are getting a divorce. We are just as normal as the kids whose parents are still married. God, please help those who have parents who are divorced.

W. J. W.
Immaculate Conception School, Jefferson City, MO

Dear God, please help me to have patience with my family. Help me most of all with my ***little brother,*** because he is the youngest in my family, and sometimes he can get a little annoying. Thank you, God, for all that you do.

Pat Leaf
Cotter Junior High School, Winona, MN

I'm not a child any more,
I can do it on my own.
I'm not an adult, yet,
I can't drive myself to school.
I need to express myself.
Were your bell-bottoms so much better than my flannel?
I like this kind of music. What's wrong with it?
I'm not a "model child." So what? Were you?
I'm not like everyone else. You needed your own identity, too.
You're too overprotective.
Did you think I'd get mugged at the mall with eight other
             people?
I need my privacy; the "knock, please" sign on my door is there
             for a reason.
I'm not trying to leave home. I just need my space.
You underestimate me.
I can pick good friends without your help.
Please try to understand.
I'm not like you; I'm like me.

Carrie Lynn Anderson
Saint Pius X Parish, Ainsworth, NE

As I walk through a field of flowers barefooted, I feel nothing
             but green grass tickle my feet.

As I smell the flowers, they tickle my nose.

As I look at the sky, I think of my dad.

It brings tears to my eyes—not tears of **sadness,** but tears of
    happiness that I had a dad like I did.

Rachel Miller
Saint John of the Cross Parish, New Caney, TX

Loving God,
We pray to you this glorious day, that you keep our pets happy and healthy. They show unconditional love for us, and we thank you for creating them this way.

We pray for those who have had pets that have died or are dying, for these are the people who truly need you. These animals are considered family, and that is why it is so hard for us when we see them hurt or aging.

We especially pray for those who have had pets that have been lost. Help these pets to find their way home.

Lastly, help all pet owners as well as pets to be safe from all harm. Amen.

Drew Meredith Lagergren
Saint Vivian School, Finneytown, OH

My Brother, My Hero

Dear God, I pray for my brother. I know he does not need my help, but he needs yours. Kids tease him for his disability— Down's syndrome. Why? I do not know. What I do know is that my brother is the most loving, caring, most determined boy that I have ever known. He may not be able to learn as fast as I, but he loves twice as fast. Please help him through his life, and reward him for forgiving and loving. He is my hero, and if any- thing were to happen to him, I would be very regretful for not asking you to help him through the everyday hardships in his life. Thank you. Amen.

Stacy
Saint Ephrem Parish, Sterling Heights, MI

Dear God,

Please hear my prayer to help my family and my friends stay safe and in good health. Please help them to live their life to the fullest and to enjoy every moment they can. God, I am grateful for everything you have given me. My family is most important in my life. I am very thankful for them. Even though sometimes I don't show it, I really love them.

Clint McKinley
Saint Dominic Parish, Sigel, PA

I'm feeling very sad God, for my father has died, and I do not know what to think. My heart aches with sadness, and I miss him so much. But then again I know when a person dies, they really arise. I know he's in heaven with you,

    where joy never ends,
    where people never die,
    and where life is a beatitude.

Knowing this makes me realize that death is just a beginning, not a dead end but a start—a start to something so great we can never fathom it. To know that my father is there lifts my sorrow and puts happiness in its place. All I can say is that I will hope and pray, that someday I will be there with you and my father.

Cameo Konfrst
Saint Cletus School, LaGrange, IL

Dear God, I wish that you could help my parents to stop fighting. They always talk about getting divorced when they argue. Sometimes my mom takes off her ring and gives it back to my dad. When she leaves the house, my dad calls her on the phone and tells her to come back home. She does. Then when my dad comes home from work, she talks about leaving again. Can you please help them? Thank you, God. I really feel bad when they fight. Amen.

Brent DeMarco
Saint Michael School, Livonia, MI

I am thankful for my family who loves and cares for me. I **love** and **cherish** every moment that I spend with them. They cheer me up when I am down. I switch to a smile from a frown. God, I want to pray for them and everything they do. Love and care for them like they care for me. I love my family, my God. Protect them with your power. Amen.

Dusty Francis
Saint Remy Parish, Russia, OH

Dear God, I want to thank you for taking my grandma where she wants to be—where she will be watched all the time, and where she will be with someone she loves. She has a very *strong golden heart.* And for always, please, God, watch over me forever. Amen.

Staci Dawn Comes
Our Lady of Lourdes School, Porcupine, SD

Every day I used to wake up and think, "Oh, it's a new day." Don't get me wrong, I loved life, but I did not fully appreciate each day. Now, because of my father's cancer, I have awakened to the joy of life. Never would I have thought that my father would be taking "chemo." Things like that only happened to people in the movies, not me. My dad was hardly ever sick.

Every day I now fully understand the gift of life and how fragile it really is. I thank God for every day. Also, I thank God for the success my dad is having with his medications.

I guess I should look upon my dad's illness as a blessing in disguise. Not many people get to realize and change their lives based upon how good it is just to be alive.

Name withheld
Immaculate Heart of Mary School, Atlanta, GA

A Prayer from an Adopted Child

Dear God, I know I was loved by the person who gave me life, but why go searching for her? She obviously wanted me to be loved by a family that could provide a home and a stable life. There is no reason to even call her my "birth mom." A mother is a person who watches your first steps, sees you off to the bus, and follows the bus to school the first day to make sure you're okay. A mother reads to you when you're sick, gives advice when you need it, and comforts you when you don't make the team. Thank you, God, for giving me a mother who does all these things, even if she didn't bring me into this world.

Morgan Ashley O'Leary
Saint Bridget School, Richmond, VA

Dear God, thank you.

Thank you for your guidance and protection during these strained and difficult times in my life.

Dear God, thank you.

Thank you for my family and the love that binds us. Thank you for the protection that you give us as you watch over and show care for us.

Thank you for my ability to lie in bed at night and cry, thinking how lucky I am to have them. And I believe that you will continue to observe and affect our lives as we grow and learn as one.

Dear God, thank you.

Conrad J. Laskowski
Saint Benedict School, Holmdel, NJ

Dear God,
I know I get in fights with my brother and sister. But sometimes they can get really annoying. But when I do hurt them, I feel bad. Seeing the looks on their faces makes me think of how they look up to me, and how I just broke their trust.

So please help me to do the right thing when I am frustrated with them, and please forgive me for what I have done. But please help them to do the right thing also. Amen.

Tom A. Ries
Regina Elementary School, Iowa City, IA

Dear God,

Thank you for letting me have arms to come home to.

When I wake up in the morning, they are there to greet me.

When I am sad, those arms care for me and make me happy.

When I am cold, I know they will be there ready to warm me up.

When I am mad, those arms are always there to cheer me up.

When I am wounded, they will hold me and heal me.

When I am happy, they will be there to laugh with me.

When I am sick, they will be beside me, holding me.

Those arms are the arms that belong to my mother.

Thank you so much, God.

April Snow
Saint Theresa Parish, Oakland, ME

Dear God,

Bless all the animals, for they are living, too.

They eat and sleep and play, just like me and you.

Bless their home and habitat that they may live in peace.

Bless their scales and fur, and even their feathers and fleece.

Please, dear God, bless all the animals of this earth.

And **may they have a wonderful life,** from the first day of their birth.

C. M.
Saint Wendelin School, Butler, PA

Good Morning, God!
Thank you for letting me see another day.
Thank you for taking care of my mom and letting me go to
church every Sunday. Even though I miss my mom,
I know you are taking care of her. I know she is
watching me all the time. Thank you for letting me
spend twelve years with her, and thank you for letting
me still be alive. My dad and I miss her, but we know
you are taking care of her.
God is taking care of all of us.
God loves us, and God has angels all around us.

Preston Colby Spivey
Nativity of Our Lady Mission Parish, Darien, GA

God has given us each a gift that should be used to the
best of our ability. I feel that God has blessed me with
patience. I have a brother with Down's syndrome who needs
help doing certain tasks. I am someone he can count on
to help him. Sometimes people get frustrated with him, but
I can be calm. I enjoy being with him and helping him.
I listen when others tune him out. Many people miss the
beauty of the world because they don't have patience. I pray
that I can keep this special gift, and that I somehow find
the strength to be patient, even on bad days. I thank
God whenever I can and ask for God's help.

Matthew Roff
Immaculate Conception Parish, Stony Point, NY

Part 4

God Is in the Hard Times

Dear God,

My heart is **broken,** and my life is *torn.* I shall not live the life I lived before. Sadness of this size will not pass. I know the scar will not grow less. Rejected by all, both love and friend, *my life is over.* My soul is dead. Forgive me, God. Amen.

Joseph Iesue
Saint George School, Erie, PA

Oh, God, I pray to you because I'm hurt.
People like to make fun of me.

 I **really need** your help.

Give me the strength to ignore them.
Thank you, almighty God.

Jeff Hicks
Cathedral of Saint Raymond Parish, Joliet, IL

Dear God,
Help me to be strong. Each day as we go through life, it's hard. People make fun of us, we get laughed at, we all get in fights, and at the end of the day, we all feel really bad about ourselves. Sometimes it is hard to go on. God, please give me the strength to carry on each day. Make me a better person so that I don't always have to say such mean things about other people. It hurts them, and it hurts me. I don't know why I say those mean things. Amen.

Wittney Sprigg
Holy Trinity School, Louisville, KY

Dear God,

Here I stand, in front of you, asking you to forgive me for all the things I have done that are not truthful or right, for all the times I have disobeyed my parents. Forgive me for eating candy before dinner, ice cream for breakfast, and drinking pop instead of milk. Forgive me for being negative.

Forgive me for every time I yelled at my sister, got mad at my parents. Forgive me for eating popcorn and caramel with my braces on.

Bottom line, God, forgive me for everything I have ever done that I should not have, especially when I knew not to do it. Help me to start anew every day. Amen.

Catherine DeSarno
Saint Agnes School, Springfield, MO

Dear God,

The world is so confusing, a crossword puzzle of life. There are so many temptations that we just can't withstand. So many questions we want to ask, but can't. So many answers we need to know to get through this life.

We are pressured into sinning, snickering, and lying about you. I know I'm not the perfect Christian, but I try my best, I do. We need to be guided along by a bright, shining light. We must try to be strong; please uphold us when we fall.

Give us hope and send us through our day. Give us the strength we need to dodge the arrows of the week. Give us understanding to communicate with ease. Give us courage to face the world today. Give us perseverance to never give up. And give us humbling moments to thank you as we should.

Thank you, God, for helping us to succeed and giving us the most wonderful gift . . . LIFE!

Meghan L.
FACES Middle School, Fond du Lac, WI

Life can sometimes be too much to handle alone.
We often need someone to listen to us.
Not criticize, or answer, or even talk.
Just to listen, and when we're finished talking, try to help.
But it usually seems as if this type of person does not exist.
Many times we just sit and sulk, waiting for the right person to
        come along.
Most of the time we do not even realize that this person has
        been here the whole time.
This person listens, and in his own silent way, really seems to
        help.
God.
With God on our side, we can get through anything the world
        can throw at us.
Us and God.
We make a great team in the game of life.

Michele Milano
Saint Richard School, Philadelphia, PA

Oh, Jesus, we love you and praise you. During your life you
were blessed with two parents who cared for you and loved
you. Help those who have lost a parent or have difficult family
issues. During your earthly life you must have known the
despair of some young adults who felt their life was worth
nothing. Please help those who are confused in their life, for
you know what it is like to live on this earth, to know of the
hardships that we all face in our everyday lives. Give strength
to anyone who may fall along the roadside or stumble through
dark paths. May you be their light to show them the way, and
may they feel the love of God for them. Amen.

Jacob Abdo
Annunciation School, Minneapolis, MN

Dear God,

Sometimes I don't know why you're doing these things to me. It seems as though you've made my river much rougher than everyone else's. Sometimes it's hard for me to keep trusting that maybe you really do know what you're doing and that you do understand.

Oh, God, help me to keep my faith strong. I know—somewhere deep inside me—that you are all good and would never really want to hurt me. It is my choices that are doing this, and you brought it on for a reason that I cannot yet see. Help me to follow where your river takes me, and to always try my best to keep my ship afloat. I know it may be hard, but with you at my side, I can make it through it all. Amen.

Sarah Part
Incarnation School, Centerville, OH

God,

I pray for everyone in the world who has been **rejected** sometime in their life. I pray that they will find somebody to accept them. And I pray that everybody who has ever rejected someone else will see that what they are doing is **wrong.**

Alex Richey
Our Lady of Sorrows Parish, Monroe, OH

Dear God,

Everyone talks about me. I don't know whether they talk good or bad about me. I'm too shy to ask. How come I couldn't have been smarter? Or cooler? How come I couldn't be rich like them? **Why God, why?**

Audrey Anne de Guzman
Saint Anne School, Houston, TX

Dear God,

Everything is frustrating, and I need you to forgive me. There are times I feel I can't handle it, and I just need a time of peace to sit and be comfortable with myself and others. I feel alone sometimes, even when people are telling me that you are everywhere. I feel deserted, and the only one I can talk to is you. *Show me peace* through your love. Amen.

Annie FitzSimmons
Saint Joseph Parish, Good Thunder, MN

Dear God,
Life is hard sometimes, and I don't know where to turn. With your help though, I think I can make it. You are always there for anyone who needs help, even me. Please hear me now. I need your help. I don't think I can make it by myself.

Patrick A. Bartenstein
Holy Trinity School, Louisville, KY

God, thank you very much for what you have provided—family, friends, a house, teachers, and school. Despite all I am grateful for, I still need your help. . . . I need tolerance and patience with my family and teachers. I need help to resist jealousy. I need strength to live in today's world and still be a good person. Please continue filling all my needs in life, and help conquer my weaknesses and fears.

Hillary Richard
Cotter Junior High School, Winona, MN

Dear God,
Sometimes I just feel like the whole world is stepping on me.
Life has been so tough at school as well as at home. Please
help me.

Angie Theis
Saint Matthias School, Chicago, IL

I pray that NOTHING will go bad,
and the house I live in will not be broken into,
and my dad and stepmom will still be home.

Stacy Renea Mustacato
Precious Blood Parish, Trotwood, OH

Divorce

Why do I feel this way?
They were together,
And now they are worst enemies.
I feel like I have to pick sides.
It hurts so much.
The pain never leaves.
It is always hanging over me.
Why do things like this happen?
People say it gets better.
I say, WHEN?

I believe in myself.
I believe in God.
I know God is there to help me.
Things will get better.

Joshua Messier
Saint Robert School, Shorewood, WI

God help me to do what is right.
To make me a good person, you have done so much for me,
        and I thank you for that.

God, I want to be closer to you.
I feel so lost and confused. I don't know what to do.
Please help me for the rest of my life to do what is right, and
        know what is wrong. Amen.

Vanessa Vlcek
Saint Joan of Arc Parish, Lisle, IL

When it is dark and there's no light,

When you're scared and full of fright,

Jesus is with you day and night.

Do not forget this, and your life will be bright.

Erin M. Carr
Saint Therese of the Little Flower School, Cincinnati, OH

God, you are all powerful and all knowing. Everything comes from you. When I asked for forgiveness, you forgave me. When I was troubled, you gave me confidence and courage to help me make it through the hard times. When I was lost, you showed me the light. When I needed a friend, you were there for me. When I had to make a tough decision, you helped me to stand up for what was right. Oh, God, by your words and actions, you have told me never to give up, but instead come to you and you will take care of my every need. Amen.

Kevin Frey
Saint Louis School, Memphis, TN

Are you there God? I know you are, but sometimes I wonder. I know they say you carry me through my hard times, and that you walk next to me through the good times, but sometimes my legs hurt. Please help me, God, give me strength when my journey feels long and my legs feel as though they can't go on. Give me the strength to walk on my own and carry myself through the rough times. Give me the strength not only to know that you are with me but to know you have always been with me. Remind me, oh, God, that your love for me is unconditional and is greater than I can imagine. Help me to love as you love me.

Emily
Villa Maria School, Erie, PA

God made me special and unique, therefore I am a gift. God gave me talents, which at times I don't use. Sometimes I become upset with myself because God knows that I can do better; but, I still have my doubts. It sometime scares me to think that I doubt God.

Many times I think God is calling me, but I shut God off and turn away. I wonder, how can I turn away from my Creator, the one who made me, and loves me the most?

Many times I reflect about what it would be like to have self-confidence and not depend on others for encouragement. I think God tries to help enhance my self-esteem. Sometimes I feel like running into my room, locking the door, and hiding under a blanket. I just want to be alone with myself, not the me I pretend to be. Maybe if I do this I will believe that I am truly unique and special in my own way.

Melissa Caramico
Saint Bernadette School, Brooklyn, NY

Lonely, hoping to find a friend.
Oppressed and put down without end.
Reaching out yet rejected.
Deep inside innocent yet suspected.

Homeless, dreading winter ahead.
Endlessly wanting a nice, warm bed.
Longing for something more to life.
Plighted by hunger, pain, or strife.

Turning sadly in the wrong way.
Hopelessly waiting for a better day.
Only one to stand up for you.
Sightless, wanting to see anew.
Entering a lonely state of depression.

Waiting for someone to hear their confession.
Hurriedly helping a friend to flee.
Only one left in the family tree.

Always knowing you're up there.
Rejected, oppressed, yet knowing you care.
Everyone will at some time find your justice. Help us have
faith.

Colleen Suzanne Reid
Incarnation School, Centerville, OH

God, life is like a mountain, where you might have to climb
steep cliffs or watch out for rocks tumbling down at
you.
God, shield me from the falling rocks. Help me to deal with
those who hurtle mean words and cause me to
stumble.

God, send a rope to help me climb the steep cliffs. Give me
comfort and strength to go through tough times.
God, when I come to rough waters, let me cross the quiet and
shallow streams. Help me find solutions when I have
tough problems.
God, when I reach the top of the mountain, the only person I
wish to see is you. When I die take my soul into your
hands and let me be with you in heaven.

Maddie Haigh
Saint Patrick School, Brighton, MI

God, when I fall and can't get up, lift me up and let me stand.
Fill me with the strength to continue.

When I fail to reach my goal, pick me up and encourage me.
Lead me to my best.

When I am filled with fear, guide me through rough times.
Fill me with the courage to be brave.

When I am weak, make me strong.
Protect me from danger and be my shield.

When I am lost and worried, show me the way.
Be the light that shines my path.

When temptation fills me, help me fight.
Help me to make the right decision.

As I continue my journey through life, God, be my faith and
my truth, so that I can fulfill my mission as your child from
heaven. Amen.

Hilda Marie Loria
Santa Barbara School, Dededo, Guam

Please, God, let me have the strength to go on in life. Sometimes I don't feel like doing anything but lying in bed. Help me to find your love so that I may continue growing spiritually. Also, guide me to whatever vocation you want me to go to. Help me help other people through my strengths, and help me let other people help me through my weaknesses.

Matt Mlinar
Father Marquette Middle School, Marquette, MI

God, oh, God, why can't I get it?
I try and try, but it doesn't come.
I am doing everything right,
Trying not to get frustrated,
But it doesn't come.
I can't land it.
I can't get it to stay together.
I can't get it to work,
But I still try.
And with your help,
Nothing will bring me down.
So, God, I ask you,
Help me through this.
Help me succeed.
I will land it.
It will stay together.
It will work.
I will try.

E. J. Marcinizyn
Saint Hedwig School, Wilmington, DE

Part 5

God Is in the Whole World

We are all a piece of a jigsaw puzzle. We are all great in value because without someone we will never finish the puzzle— the puzzle of **LIFE.** One day we all will find our place in the puzzle. Everyone will see what the puzzle is and see that without one person we can't finish.

Joe Nolan
Saint James Parish, Cazenovia, NY

God,
We pray for ourselves, growing up in an unsteady and confusing
        world.
Show us that following you is better then chasing after our selfish
        goals.
Help us to take failure not as an end but as a new start.
Give us strength to hold our faith in you, and to keep alive our
        joy in your creation.
Amen.

Gabe Estes
Blanchet School, Salem, OR

Dear God,
Please help all of those who are having troubles. Help the
kids who need someone to listen to their personal problems.
Especially, dear God, help children who are at schools where
there are hate crimes and shootings. I also pray for those who
are sick, injured, frightened, worried, lonely, or hungry. Amen.

Erin Ashley Grant
Saint Patrick Parish, Troy, OH

Dear God,

You have given me so much to be grateful for, most of all my mom who chose to give me life. Please change the hearts of women who think abortion is their only solution. Make them know they're carrying a life in their womb. Give them the strength and understanding to admit that abortion is murder. Help the women to treat the baby as the life it is.

Help the men involved to stand up and support what they know is right. Please change the hearts of the doctors who perform abortions. Show them they are just as wrong as the women choosing abortion.

God, thank you for my mom, and please bless all the aborted babies and all moms who choose life. Amen.

Kathleen McKinnon
Saint John School, Westminster, MD

Dear God,

I am offering a prayer to you today asking for guidance in using my talents. Sometimes I am not willing to share my gifts with others. When this happens, my entire community is missing out on something special. Help me to use the unique gifts you have given me to work with others, trying to make the world a better, more loving place. God, by doing simple things, like smiling or saying hi when passing someone, holding a door, doing a task before being told, and treating others like I would like to be treated, I am becoming your instrument of service. Help me to put my whole mind, heart, and soul into serving you in the community around me. Amen.

Emily
Saint John Regional School, Concord, NH

I have never really known peace. Our whole world seems to constantly be at war. I will always remember . . .

> . . . the Kosovar refugees searching for their homes and their lives;
>
> . . . victims of school shootings, running away from what used to be so everyday, but is now a place of terror;
>
> . . . babies found dead in dumpsters, without a life ever led.

What happened to all the acts of love and goodwill? They seem to get lost in a whirlwind of hateful confusion. To return to the tranquillity we once knew, we all have to work together toward a just and equal world.

Laura Schultz
Saint Matthew Middle School, Wausau, WI

Dear God,

I am asking you to help the poor, but who are the poor? Are they the people with little money, or are they the people without love for you? The people without much money but with love for you are the richest people in the world. The people with a lot of money but with no true love for you are the poorest people in the world. So, God, I ask you to take care of the poor people of the world, whoever they truly are. Amen.

Chris Carino
Our Lady of the Rosary School, Greenville, SC

Dear God,
Please help all those women who are thinking about abortion to consider putting their babies up for adoption. Then their babies would be *lucky like me.* Amen.

Caitlin M. Barney
Saint Christopher School, Vandalia, OH

We all have lied, because we are human.

We all have cheated, because we are human.

We all have made bad judgments, because we are human.

We all have not excepted others, because we are human.

We all LOVE EACH OTHER, because we are human.

Megan Elizabeth Gariety
Saint Remy Parish, Russia, OH

Dear God, help me live a peaceful life. Guide me to continue to blossom as a peacemaker. Help me realize the pain and suffering of others so I may do whatever is needed to be done, to help bring peace to others. Open my eyes to all of the injustices on earth. There are times when I try not to notice suffering because I don't want to recognize all of the people who live in poverty, in fear, and in loneliness. Open my eyes to the cry of all people who have not found peace within themselves. It is they who are in most need of your love.

 I am your humble servant, God. Help me to follow Christ's footsteps so that I, too, may do your will. Amen.

Luis Sanchez
Saint Sebastian School, Santa Paula, CA

Dear God,
How can I be a better person on this earth and fulfill your hopes for us? There is so much hate in this world, and because of that I feel a huge need to help as much as I can, as long as I can, forever and ever. Amen.

Andrea Aguayo
Saint Hugh Parish, Coconut Grove, FL

Oh, dear God, we are oh so young; help us not to ruin our lives
by doing drugs.
Oh, dear God, protect us from violence; we are oh too young.
Oh, dear God, help us stay healthy; we are oh too young.
Oh, dear God, be by our side because we are the next
generation to rule the world, and I don't want the
world to be ruined.
Oh, dear God, make us smart so we can make the world a
better place.
Oh, dear God, don't ruin this generation.
Oh, dear God, let us chase our dreams.

Courtland J. Hathaway
Saint Charles Borromeo School, Syracuse, NY

Dear God,
Remember all the babies in their mothers' wombs.
All the children crying in their rooms.
The homeless who have called out in fear,
Help them know that you are near.
Please, God, forgive all of our sins,
Even the ones we hold deep within.
Thank you for my family and friends,
I know you'll stay with me until the end.
Thank you for listening to my prayer,
And also for always being there.

Brianne R. Dondlinger
Saint Thomas Aquinas School, Wichita, KS

Almighty God,

Hear the cries of the victims of violence. Find a place of peace for those who are troubled and in harm's way. Let those whose violence has roots in addiction to harmful substances seek help before they hurt others. May those who have guns not be tempted to use them in a manner that could inflict harm unto others or themselves. Please prevent prejudice and hate, for they are the causes of most violence.

We are your **frightened children** who long for your peace. Please bring it to all of your servants here on earth and protect us from harm and violence. Amen.

Your troubled daughter,

Anne Augustine
Saint Gregory the Great School, Williamsville, NY

Please, God,
Enable us to be
At peace with all
Creation for
Ever and always. Amen.

Erica M. Rugis
Holy Rosary School, Claymont, DE

God, you have given me so many gifts—my family, my friends, a house to live in, food to eat, a school to go to, and so much more. And for these things I am grateful. But I also have a family with problems, friends with fear, people with no homes to live in, no food to eat, or no school to go to. For these I have been given my most precious gift of all, the gift to share.

Lauren Doherty
Saint John Fisher School, Chicago, IL

Reach out to other people
Enrich others' lives
Share faith
Protect others
Establish relationships
Care for the less fortunate
Talk things over

Mrs. Salyer's seventh grade religious education class
Saint Mary Parish, Bluffton, OH

My God in heaven,
I'm grateful for what you have given me, but I don't always understand your ways. You are a God of praise, joy, love, and understanding, yet in this world we find sorrow, suffering, poverty, and hatred. I ask you and I ask myself,

"Why?"

If you don't mind, would you please help me to understand your ways, so I can show others. Amen.

Megan Deaton
Pope John XXIII School, Middletown, OH

God, let everyone know they are loved, wanted, and cared for,
That they are not alone in the world.
> Let them know you care.
For people who are suffering from hunger, disease, or loneliness,
> Let them know you are there.
For those who wrong others, that they try to make it right,
> Let them know you forgive them.
For the people who are sick,
> Let them know that you will do what is right for them.
For the people who have died,
> may they be happy and look after us here on earth.
God, for all your people, whether kind, hateful, loving, or
> deceitful,
> look after us, and guide us to your kingdom.
For everyone, even though they may not know it, belongs to you.

Katie Parrish
Saint Francis of Assisi School, Baltimore, MD

Oh, my Jesus, please help us to pray for those who are sick, lonely, and abandoned, that they find their own eternal happiness.

Oh, my Jesus, please help us to pray for the sinners, the grievers, and the unbelievers, that they find true hope and happiness in you.

Oh, my Jesus, please help us to pray for the souls aborted, the souls rewarded, and the souls tormented, that in the next life they reach happiness.

Oh, my Jesus, please help us to pray for the people of the world each and every one, the good and the bad, the poor and the rich, that we all find happiness in this life and the next.

Shannon Hollander
Saint Peter School, Saint Charles, MO

Dear God,
Thank you for every day that I live and walk and breathe. I can't thank you enough for everything that you've done for me. I feel that I am different from others, for I know that you have a special plan for me. I know that I will do something different in your name on this planet. Every time I ask you about something, I know that you will help me.

So now I am asking you to help me **make a difference** in this world.

Valerie
Saint Anne School, Memphis, TN

Who will I love?
What will I learn?
Where will I travel?
God only knows the answer.
I sit as still as night waiting for a hope of seeing the earth's wild
        beauty.
The time is right to go into the world.
I see only for an instant the busy life I would have led.
Then, my life is snuffed out like a candle.

God, save my unborn brothers and sisters.
Let them emerge from their mothers' wombs into the light of life.
Their only wish is to be born without the shadow of a knife
        waiting to strike at their innocent lives.
Let men and women repent and be forgiven.
Let them realize that every child has the right to life.
This is the only wish left for me to wish.
Amen.

Colleen M. Forst
Saint John School, Westminster, MD

Part 6

God Is Part of It All

When I need you, you are there.
But when I don't, you still care.
I like you for all the things you do.
God, I wish I were you!
You make your life sound very easy,
But I know it is hard taking care of me.
So I try to thank you night and day.
But sometimes I just don't know what to say.
I hate it when you're hard on me,
And sometimes I get very angry.
I know you are just trying to help,
Because there are some things I cannot do by myself.
I know it when you are there,
Because there is a feeling in the air.
I hope you come again and again.
Thank you, God, for being my friend.

Bobby Rarick
Saint Frances Cabrini Parish, Hoxie, KS

I think about all I've done,

received,

given,

and tried to do.

You have been there to watch me.

Be there *again* and *forever.*

Amen.

Maria-Theresa Peralta
Saint John Vianney Parish, Rancho Cordova, CA

Dear God,

You made the day and the night, *just for us.*

You made the stars and the moons, *just for us.*

You have given us light to shine through the world, *just for us.*

You sacrificed your life to save us from sin, *just for us.*

Now we will do what is right, *just for you!*

Amen.

Alex Greenwell
Saint John the Baptist School, Silver Spring, MD

Dear Lord, my one and only God,
Help me to assist or help you and others.
Help me to prove what I can and cannot do.
Help me to overcome my fears.
Protect me from danger and trouble.
Guide me through worry and sorrow.
Protect me from evil.
That is all I ask.

But most of all give me a home—a home in heaven,
Where I can be loved by you and others,
Even in times of sadness and darkness,
In times of peace and war.
Let me know that people care.
That is all I ask.

My life is not complete unless you're there,
To give me knowledge to know what is right,
To give me strength to stick up for others,
To give me courage to explore my mind,
To give me a place where I belong.
That is all I ask.

Katie Marie Webb
Saint Francis de Sales School, Salisbury, MD

As rolling clouds go passing by
I see an image of your face
As vague as it may seem to me
I feel the power of your grace

In times of deep sorrow
And in times of deep pain
You spread your wings and lifted me
And sheltered me through the rain

Never once have I doubted you
Never once did you let me down
Which led me to believe
That you will always be around

And so I say this prayer today
That you share your special love
With the ones who are dear to me
My angel from above

Imee P. Fajardo
Santa Barbara School, Dededo, Guam

I like to think of your love as a slide,
A slide upon which we may ride.
A slide that never will give way.
A slide that always likes to say:
"I'll love you as much as I can love.
I'll never push. I'll never shove.
When you feel sad or lonely,
Just grab a hold! Hang on to me.
You'll skid, you'll slide, you'll even slip!
But hang on tight! Don't loose your grip!"
I like to think of your love as a giant slide,
A slide upon which we may ride.

Emily Butler
Saint Jerome School, Maplewood, MN

Oh, God, you love me *because I am me.*

You loved me when I was hurt.

You loved me when I broke my arms.

You loved me when I was heartbroken.

You carried me when I fell.

God, you do these things *because you are all good.*

Justin Michael Veith
Gesu School, Toledo, OH

Dear God,
When I was crying, you sent crickets to sing me to sleep.
When I was upset, you sent friends so I should not weep.
When I was lonely, you sent family to care.
Whenever I'm sad, God, you'll always be there.
When I was smiling, you sent the sun to make even brighter
        my day.
When I was lost, you sent parents and teachers to send me on
        my way.
Whenever I'm laughing, you send buddies to share my fun.
Oh, glorious God, you are the only one.
You help me.
    You heal me.
        You love me.
            You care.
        You forgive me.
    You respect me.
You are always there.
To the maker of forests, and birds that sing,
Thank you, God, for everything.
I love you. Amen.

Erin E. Esposito
Saint Therese School, Succasunna, NJ

God,
I have a question.
How is it that my troubles seem so big, yet I am so small?
When my plans change, it's such a big deal to me.
But when I look back on it, I think,
"How could I be so upset? I am so small, and my troubles are
        smaller."
But I am part of creation,
part of this world.
I count.
I matter.
I have my answer.

Emma Lueger
Saint Robert School, Shorewood, WI

Dear God,

It is you who I think of all the time, wondering all about you,

Wondering if you could watch me today,

To make sure I'm okay.

And in response I will pray to you every day,

I will love you forever,

And one day I will see you again.

Stephanie
Our Lady of the Sacred Heart School, Orchard Park, NY

I do not think it is true that only insects and birds can fly.
I think that the soul can fly too.

   And if the soul can fly, there will be **peace.**
I think the heart can fly too.

   And if the heart can fly, there will be **friendship.**
I also think the mind can fly.

   And if the mind can fly, there will be **love.**

Ashley Johnson
Saint Pascal Baylon School, Saint Paul, MN

Dear God, I walk alone in dark halls.
Some days I take great falls.
I walk through painful meadows,
and a thousand spikes touch my toes.
I run around and around,
for nowhere am I bound.
Then God puts a hand on me
and lets me see that I don't walk alone
and I have somewhere to go.
God will help those who have been sinned against and will not
         bring revenge on those who have sinned. God will
         heal, free, and forgive those who need it.
That's what gives me courage for
walking through dark halls and
taking great falls . . .
when I need to.

Ryan Davis
Our Lady's Immaculate Heart Parish, Ankeny, IA

God, be near me always. Every day help me to make a positive impact on someone else. Help me to be kind and just to everyone I come in contact with. Give me patience when I am angry. Help me to strive to do my very best at everything I do. Teach me to take life one step at a time, and help me to enjoy life and live it to its fullest. Don't let me grow up too quickly. Protect me from danger and cruelty. Guide me on the right path, which you have made for me. Help me to do what is right. Give me courage.

George H. Ganey
Saint Perpetua School, Lafayette, CA

Good morning, God. Bless me this morning and make my day a good day and let no harm come to me. Help me in school; help me remember what I should do or not do, and help me remember to speak English, and that's all I need. Amen.

Daniel Collado
Nativity of Our Lady Mission Parish, Darien, GA

The light is so bright and warm. It is **overwhelming** and **so welcoming.** I walked in and felt your power, God.

Thank you.

Jenny
Saint Matthias School, Chicago, IL

When I am made fun of, because of my faith,
    help me to remember Saint Stephen, who died for his faith.
When I am in pain,
    help me to remember how Jesus died on the cross to save
        us.
When I sin,
    help me to remember Adam and Eve.
When I am afraid to lead,
    help me to remember how Moses led the slaves out of
        Egypt, to be free.
When I make fun of others because they are different,
    help me to remember that Jesus was different, too.
When I feel that I can't take one more step,
    help me to remember the three times that Jesus fell on his
        way up Calvary Hill.
When I am mad at my siblings,
    help me to remember Joseph, and how he forgave his
        brothers after they threw him in a dry well.
When I feel that no one is on my side,
    help me to remember how Jesus felt when he was being
        tortured to death.
When I am tempted,
    help me to remember the three temptations Jesus faced in
        the desert.
When I need love,
    help me to remember you, God.
Amen.

Angela Pistorio
Saint Joseph School, Fullerton, MD

God,
> You love us.
> You help us.
> You gave us your word.
>> We love you.
>> We praise you.
>> We live your word.
>>> We need you.
>>> We sing to you.
>>> We spread your word.

David Fournier
Ladyfield Catholic School, Toledo, OH

Dear God,
Sometimes I wonder if you are real or if there is a heaven. I get scared of dying, but I know you're with me, so I don't have anything to worry about.

God, I thank you for my life and my family's lives, the animals you created, the trees, sky, moon, stars, and your Son. Help me make the right choices and follow in your footsteps. Amen.

Logan Peltier
Piqua Catholic School, Piqua, OH

This day is **one of a kind.**
I realize that God.
Please help me not to waste it, but seize it.
God in heaven, shine on me just today,
Because today is one of a kind. Amen.

Evan L. McCarley
Saint Anne School, Houston, TX

Dear God,

You are my shepherd who guards me always. You listen when I need to talk and give advice though you do not speak. When life gets to be too much and I stray from your love, you gently call me back. You teach me to be fair and make me understand that what I want is not always what is good for me. **The bottom line,** God, is you're my best friend. Amen.

Katie James
Owensboro Middle School, Owensboro, KY

Dear God,
Thank you for the morning light, the sun that shines so high
    and bright.
Give us the courage and strength to do, everything that pleases
    you.
Guide us through each darkened day, and help us to live by
    your Son's way.
You grant us so many wishes and beautiful things, so let us be
    thankful for all that life brings.
Even though there are many unjust things about, your love and
    guidance I will never doubt.
Help us to be good in all that we do, and help our lives to reflect
    you.
God, you are the stronghold of our lives, hear us through our
    joys and cries.
Keep us close to your side, and become our never-ending guide.
God, wash out the evils in my heart, and never let anything draw
    us apart.
Help us not to fight and destroy, but let us share in others' joy.
Someday when my time is done, I will rejoice with you and
    your Son.

M. M.
Saint Michael School, Livonia, MI

Dear God,
Sometimes I'm happy, sometimes I'm not.
　　　You always help me get over my tears.
Sometimes I pray, sometimes I forget.
　　　But you will always be in my heart.
Sometimes I'm scared, sometimes I'm brave.
　　　You help me get over all of my fears.
Sometimes I sin, sometimes I don't.
　　　But you forgive me either way.
Sometimes I don't love others like I should.
　　　But I will always love you. Amen.

Chasity G. Dodd
Saint Catherine of Siena School, Metairie, LA

Dear God, I'm ready for bed, and I thought I would say good-night and thank you for all of my blessings—the food I received and the love of family and friends. Before I fall asleep I wanted to ask you to **watch over me** and those I love. Amen.

Megan McClure
Sacred Heart Parish, Lacey, WA

Dear God,
I may not have been the best Christian lately, and I'm asking your forgiveness. I know I don't have a good relationship with you—if any relationship at all—but I would like to have a relationship with you if you would help me start it. Thanks for everything you've given me.

Arielle
Saint Thomas More School, Baton Rouge, LA

Abba,

Snowflakes truly are a gift from above. They fall so swiftly and peacefully. Not a single one of them is alike, and they are all beautiful. When snow falls it is so perfect and white, until people tamper with it by splashing mud on it with their cars, and make it become "ugly."

God, you made snowflakes as a reminder to humans that we are all unique and not a single person is the same, just like snowflakes. We, too, are also perfect in your image until people around us tamper with us and make us "ugly." No person on this earth is "ugly" because we are made in your image, and GOD IS.

God, what I ask of you today is for a little extra guidance and reassurance to remind us that we are beautiful. Amen.

Michelle Smits
Holy Name of Jesus School, Kimberly, WI

Jesus, you help us in our time of need.
You care for and love us, no matter what.
Our love for you is as precious to us as anything else.

A friend, that is what you are. You're with us through thick and
        thin.
When we need someone, you are there.
When we are sad and lonely, you are there.

A caring friend, that is what you are.
You are the center of our lives.
The time we have with you is our greatest time.
We love and care for you, and we know you are our

LORD JESUS CHRIST!

Tom Gruber
Saint Antoninus School, Cincinnati, OH

Dear God,
What have I done to deserve your wonderful love? When people say that they can't see or touch you, I feel this cannot be true. Who has looked at a beautiful sunset and not felt the awe of your presence? Who has been given a hug and not felt you there? How can anyone say that you cannot be felt, for I feel you every day. Your love is what makes me get up each morning, and feel secure at night. If it is true that you live in us, then who can say that you have left us all alone here. For this feeling of your presence, I thank you and give you all of my love.

Vicky Gayle Becerra
Holy Family School, North Miami, FL

Hi, God!

Help me get through this day,

Through every thought and every way.

Don't let me be hurt by what others think,

I know the day goes by in a wink!

Don't let me yell, or tell others what to do,

I might already be doing that. (To just a few!)

I might always want to win,

But as you know, cheating is a sin.

You did a great job,

creating many marvelous thingamabobs.

Maggie Hediger
Saint Agnes School, Springfield, MO

You made the tree; you made the flower.
You made all things; you have the power.
You made the sun;
You made its rays.
You made all things in seven days.
You made Adam; you made Eve,
You let them come; you made them leave.
I'm thankful that you made all these,
But most of all that you made me!

Mary Casey
Nativity School, Dubuque, IA

The Death of Jesus Christ

Judas of Iscariot wasn't really on Jesus' side.
He turned him in to the Roman guards the night before Jesus
        died.
They placed him before Pontius Pilate and whipped his back
        bright red.
They put him back before the crowd and pushed thorns deep
        into his head.
When Jesus was condemned to death, he knew that he would
        die. He looked up in the heavens and asked, "Why,
        O Father, why?"
Jesus was nailed to a cross by his hands and feet.
He was left up there to die in the extreme heat.
Nearly three hours later, Jesus looked up and said,
"Father, it is finished," and he slowly dropped his head.
That is the story of Jesus Christ. Some thought Christians were
        thinning.
Others thought it was the end, but it was only the beginning.

Michael H. Culligan
Saint James the Apostle School, Glen Ellyn, IL

Dear God,
Thank you for giving me so much and helping me immensely. Thank you for guiding me through the rough patches and walking with me in the sunlight. When I pray to you, thank you for letting me know you care by answering in one way or another. Please, after all you've done for me, help me be the absolute best person I can be—for you. Amen.

Jessica Bolack
Divine Infant Parish, Westchester, IL

The sun shining in my face.
The leaves blowing around me.
The trees swaying faster and faster.
I feel the cold wind on my face.
The branches crunching from the wind.
The birds nestled safely in their tree.
I feel I'm alone, ***but I'm not.***

Lyle Francis Robin
Saint John of the Cross Parish, New Caney, TX

Lord, give me your courage, for I cannot stand up against the
    forces that strike my soul.
Give me your will, so I can use the gifts you have given me
    confidently and wisely each and every day of my life.
Give me your love, so I can break through the shackles of
    hatred and live in love and peace.
Give me your faith, for I doubt the Almighty when things go
    wrong.
Lord, help me to live as you did. Amen.

Sam Tatel
Saint John the Evangelist School, Warrington, FL

God,
Where have you been?
When I have sinned against you.
Times I have hurt others physically or mentally.
Times I have stabbed my friend in the back.
Times when I can choose right or wrong and I do not know
what to do.
When I disobey you, a law, or rule set by one of my supervisors.
When I go to bed at night and not pray, or thank you.
God, were you there to witness these unjust acts set forth by me?
Yes, God, you were there. You saw, but you are the one who
gave us the freedom of choice. You knew all this would
happen.
I am sorry.
And I thank you, God.

Jay
Villa Maria School, Erie, PA

Oh, my God,

I love you, and you love me.

Forgive me for all my wrongs and

Please let everything always go well.

I pray that you will always be there for me.

I pray you give me **hope, joy,** surprises, and **love.**

Please let all my dreams come true and

Let my days be wonderful and my life a blessing.

Amen.

Helen Ortiz
Saint Frances Xavier Cabrini Parish, Piscataway, NJ

I don't show that I love you as much as I should,
But know that I do, my intentions are good.
I am ever so grateful for all that you've done;
You've given so much, yet taken none.
All I have is because of you;
My blessings are many, my misfortunes few.
I sometimes get busy with the happenings of the day,
And don't always take time out to pray.
Please be patient with me and guide me along;
To make good decisions, to understand right from wrong.
Dear God, remember that I love you,
And I know in my heart that you love me too.

John M. Horal
Saint Patrick School, Brighton, MI

God, I pray that you stay with me all of my life.
Guide me through good and bad.
Be there when I need to talk.
God, just please be there.

God, I pray that you will be there for me.
I pray that you steer me the right way in life.
I pray that you'll be there when I need a friend.
God, just please be there.

God, be there when I am in trouble.
I pray you're there for me morning, noon, night,
winter, spring, summer, fall.
God, just please be there.

Alayna Flynn
Father Marquette Middle School, Marquette, MI

O loving God, source of all things, you have created us in your own image so that we may be able to praise and worship you. I'm here to present myself. You didn't have to create me, but you chose to anyway, and I'm thankful for that. I believe that you have created me for a purpose, a purpose that will last all life long. Please reveal the purpose through the Holy Spirit, sent down upon me, so that I'm able to accomplish it. Amen.

Chinh Hoang
Saint Agnes Cathedral Parish, Springfield, MO

Dear Jesus,

I want to be your apostle. I want to walk in your ways.

I want to spread your word to all nations. I want to help make

the wrong right. There are many things I want to change, and

becoming closer to you may help. So today I am telling you

this from the bottom of my heart, hoping you will let me.

I want to be your apostle.

Danielle
Saint Michael Parish, Kalida, OH

Dear God,
Please show me the way to your kingdom,
Please give me the guidance so I may reach it,
Please fill me with the word of you,
And give me the **courage** to preach it.
Amen.

Eric Howe
Saint Mary of the Woods School, Whitesville, KY

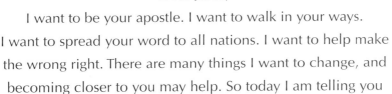

Dear God,

Help me to remember that all things, large or small, come from you, from sunsets to spring. Make me thankful for all I have, and also mindful that there are many less fortunate than I am. I must remember to share with them. Help me to find your light, which shines over me and guides me, piercing even the darkness of death.

God of all, remember that *I am only human,* and quite imperfect. I will do better next time.

Philip W. Nova
Saint Francis Solano School, Sonoma, CA

The flushing green meadows, the air that Jesus once breathed

It is a part of me.

The very place he healed us and we did not see

It is a part of me.

The salty air, the rushing river and sea

It is a part of me.

The very place Jesus forgave, and found me

He is a part of me.

Jesus and God

They are part of me.

Michelle Gallagher
Saint Joseph Parish, Force, PA

God, you are our life!
The creator of the earth.
Our reason for being here.
Everything.
You are love, hope, fidelity, and Creator.
The reason we are here right now.

Alicia Ponciano
Saint Mel School, Dearborn Heights, MI

Loving God,
Please help us to reconcile,
To strive for the impossible;
Which is to be like you.
Because we are only human,
We dismay your wishes sometimes,
But in the midst of it all
We are saved.
We have been saved
Thanks to you, my God.

We grow and aspire in a delicate world.
We are surrounded with you,
Because you created it all.
You have made beautiful people
Who love and care in your likeness;
Though not as much as you.
And we live this way
Thanks to you, my God.

Please help us to rise to that challenge;
That is, to live in your likeness.
But through it all
We know we will be all right,
Because of you, my God.

Sarah Klawinski
Saint Martin of Tours School, Buffalo, NY

Let us rejoice that God gave us life by offering his Son's.
Let us rejoice that he designed each and every one of us in
   our own unique way with his soft, natural touch and
   caring hands.
Let us rejoice and be thankful for every gift that has been given
   from loving hands into needy ones.
Let us rejoice that God has, and always will, forgive our sins
   and give us a second chance.
Let us rejoice that God is here, and will always be, to protect
   us from Satan and all his evil ways.
Let us rejoice that God is with us all,
   The sick and the healthy,
   The wise and the careless,
   The rich and the poor,
   The old and the young.
Let us rejoice, let us rejoice.

David Theisen
Saint Bridget Parish, Rochester, NY

Dear God,
Please help me do right, rather than do wrong. Do not let
me fall in the hands of evil. Prevent me from saying negative
comments to others. Let me respect others' feelings so they will
respect mine. Please help me understand that if I do right and
others do wrong to me, I should forgive them. You live in our
hearts and in our homes. You live within each and every one
of us. We worship you and love you. We give you thanks, and
we respect you. Guide me through my years here on earth and
bring me to the kingdom of heaven. Amen.

Jeffrey Hogan
Church of Saint Helen, Westfield, NJ

Prayer for a Virtuous Life

God, let me not lose faith in you. Keep me hopeful and help me love my enemies even more than I love myself.
God, turn my pride into humility, my greed into mercy, my wrath into meekness and peacemaking, my lust into purity of heart.
Help me to be charitable to the poor and wealthy in your love. Amen.

Paul Pirolli
Queen of Peace Parish, Brodheadsville, PA

Please, God, if you can hear me, listen to me.

And if you can see me, look after me.

Please, God, if you can touch me, guide me.

And if you can sense me, smile upon me.

Show me the way—

With your voice,

With your hands,

And with your light.

Katherine Janczak
Church of the Holy Spirit, Schaumburg, IL

God in heaven, please guide me through my day:
Like Jesus, help me to be kind to everyone I meet today.
Also help me to avoid my temptations, and to be forgiving.
Like Mary, support me to not turn away from you, and to always
    keep you first in my life.
Like Job, bless me with the gift of patience. Assist me with my
    problems, and help me to deal with them in a Christian
    way.
Like Noah, bless me with the strength to keep my faith,
    especially through times of sorrow and trouble.
As my day goes by, help me to appreciate and reflect your
    goodness and creation.

Franco Fabiilli
Saint Veronica School, Eastpointe, MI

Dear Jesus,

I love you. I really want to be your follower, because

I like helping people and I don't like to see anyone

hurt. I will be nice to everyone—my friends,

enemies, and students who are picked on. I will not

let anyone hurt someone else's feelings. Please give

me strength to be one of your followers.

I love you, Jesus.

Jimmy Tomola
Saint Joseph Parish, Jacksonville, FL

Always By My Side

God, so far you have been great to me. You've always followed
    through.
Now there's only one more thing I'm asking you to do.
Tomorrow I will need your help, because I have to do my best,
    Whether it's a tryout, a lesson, or a test.
I know that no matter what, O God, you're always there for me.
So again I'm asking you, my God, please keep in mind my
    needs.
I ask you, God, to stay with me so right choices I do make.
I offer what I do to you all the time that I'm awake.
So, thank you, God, for listening and being at my side.
In everything I do and say, you'll always be my guide.
With this I wrap it up for now, 'cause it's time for me to go.
And since you're with me forever, the you in me will show.
    Amen.

Joe Jost
Saint Clare of Assisi School, Ellisville, MO

Dear God,
It's Friday. It's been a very fun week, but I'm ready for the
weekend. Is that okay? I mean is it okay to want to go home?
God, this weekend is going to be fun. Please help me to be
nice to everyone, and please be with me for my game. They
say this team is big; my team is small. Please help me to have
patience with my friends and family. I know sometimes my
anger builds up, and I know that happens to others. Please
give me the right words to say to others. I know you listen to
me and that's why I talk to you. Please help me to ignore the
bright signs that lead me off the right path, and help me not to
stumble on the rocks that block my path. That is all I ask. I love
you, God. Amen.

Lauren Michael
Regina Elementary School, Iowa City, IA

In all I do,
Please help me, God.
Through the times I love,
And the ones I don't.
Help me love and trust in you,
As well as everyone and everything else.
My family and relatives,
Friends and teachers,
Help me decide what to do.
But I'd still be stuck,
If I didn't have you.
Please help me, God,
In all I do.

Daniel Woods
Cathedral of Saint Raymond Parish, Joliet, IL

Oh, holy God, hear this of me. I, a simple child who has done nothing truly amazing, seek importance. Tell me that it is **my tears** that makes the world shimmer so. Tell me that it is **my smile** that brings warmth into the world. Tell me it is **my eyes** through which light enters this world, that it is **my heart** from which love flows to all creation. Most of all reach for **my hand** and guide me through darkness and evil.

Katherine Taylor Cottle
Our Lady of the Rosary School, Greenville, SC

Dear God,
I pray to you at night,
to help me through every day,
to show me right from wrong,
to help me find the way.
Please keep me on the path,
for what I'm meant to do.
I'm trusting you with my life, God,
because I believe in you.
    Love,
    Tom

T. R. Wede
Saint Teresa Parish, Mapleton, MN

Jesus is a light for the world, like a fire burning inside.
God is a light for our mind, like knowledge waiting to be used.
The Holy Spirit is a light for our soul, like a passion waiting to
        be set free.
When they are all joined together in the sign of the cross, they
        are the light for the world.

Crissy Hollinger
Our Lady of the Angels School, Columbia, PA

God's love is like a Band-Aid.
When I am hurting, it feels like the pain will never go away.
But when my mom gives me a Band-Aid and a hug, it makes
        me feel all better. Thank you for your love, God. It's
        kind of like a big Band-Aid that makes everyone and
        everything feel a lot better.

Brenda Weber
Saint Mary Parish, West Point, NE

When I think about you, God, I know you are always there.
I have so many things to tell you, and I know you will always
        care.
I want to thank you, God, for everyone I love.
For I know you sent them from heaven up above.
I hope you will forgive me, for any wrong I've done.
God, please help me follow in the footsteps of your Son.
Thank you for a bright, new day that shines upon your creation.
I know that you made this world with kindness, love, and
        patience.
I want you to realize, that we try to obey your commands.
For I know you created this world with your loving, caring
        hands.
God, thank you for your kindness that was shown by your Son.
So I'll end with this statement . . .
God, thy will be done.

Elizabeth Riesser
Saint James of White Oak School, Cincinnati, OH

God, I know I'm not always a good Christian. Sometimes I
might even have second thoughts that you exist. But in my
mind and in my heart, I know that you exist. You watch over
me day and night.

    God, I'm thankful for my life and how I've lived it. I've
made mistakes, but, hey, who hasn't? I've loved. I've lost. I've
cried a bit. I got mad sometimes. I wish I hadn't, but I must
keep focused on the future. Though when I look into the past,
oh, God, I thank you for my second chance.

Brandon J. Taylor
Saint Bernadette School, Milwaukee, WI

Dear God,
When I did something wrong, you forgave me.
When I was in the dark, you gave me light.
When I needed you, you were there.
When I was hurt, you healed me.
When I am sad, you cheer me up.
When I die, you will let me stand beside you.
Thank you, God. Amen.

Angel Nicole Mills
Our Lady of Lourdes School, Porcupine, SD

The church is your map
Your life is the road.
You are the car.
Without the map, you have no life.
Without the map, you will get lost on the road.

Walter Dusch
Church of the Resurrection, Pittsburgh, PA

Help me through these troubled times, so there will be peace.
Help me seek answers to my questions, so there will be
        understanding.
Help me with family problems, so there will be love.
Help me find the path through life, so there will be joy.
Help me get through the death of a friend, so there will be a
        memory.
Help me to live a true faith life, so there will be light for
        everyone.
Help me finish to the end, so there will be new beginnings.
Help me, God. Amen.

Roman Martinez
Saint Roman School, Milwaukee, WI

Dear God,

Though I may act as if I don't care, I do.

Though I may act like nothing is there, there is.

Though I may act like the bad is good, it isn't.

Though I may act like I have no faith, I do.

Though the world doesn't always bring peace, it should.

Though you are always there and some people don't care, I do.

Oh, God, I do believe. And though I may not act, I think.

Amen.

Vanessa DeCesare
Saint Joseph Parish, Toronto, OH

I pray to God when I feel bad.
I pray to God whenever I'm mad.
I pray to God to help me out.
When making a decision, when I'm in doubt.
I always pray for others, too.
My mom, my dad, and my sister, too.
I pray to God every day.
I pray to God when the skies are gray.
I pray when I am on the bus.
I pray to God, I just must!
I pray before I eat,
Or even when I'm in cold sleet.
I just pray whenever I can
When I have time—a lot! Amen.

Brian Rivette
Saint Mark the Evangelist Parish, Goodrich, MI

God,

You are the needle,

I am the thread.

I'm torn and **unwinding.**

Please guide me through the eye of your needle.

Accept me as a piece of Christian thread

That is woven to make cloth for you, God.

Amen.

Katie Tunder
Saint Joseph Parish, Grafton, WI

Good Lord, I hurt somebody today and walked in my own sinful
ways. I ask you, O God up in heaven, please forgive
me.
Good Lord, if I have said your name in vain and have been
disrespectful to others, let me be the one who suffers
the consequences. I ask you, good Lord, please forgive
me.
Good Lord, if I have been thinking wicked ways or thoughts that
bring evil pleasure to mind, I ask you, please forgive
me.
Good Lord, if I have been asking for more than I need and taking
things for granted, I ask you, O God, please forgive me.
Good Lord, if I have misused people or given them bad advice
or said things to them that I don't really mean, I ask
you, O God, please forgive me.
Good Lord, forgive the sins I have confessed to you and forgive
the sins I haven't committed yet. Let me learn from all
this, but now I ask you, O God, please forgive me.

Gustavo A. Bautista
Church of the Nativity, Los Angeles, CA

Gentle Jesus, please help me through today by being by my side.

Take my hand, God, and guide me so my words or my actions

don't hurt anyone's feelings or emotions. Help me **run**

away from sin and run to prayer. Lord God, I praise you.

David Wayne Moretz Jr.
All Saints School, Burlington, NJ

I see your love in us and in everything you created.

You made us out of love,

You died for us out of love.

Thank you for my life and the lives of others.

Thank you for the bright things, and the dark.

Thank you for giving me the freedom to choose what's right
            and wrong.

Thank you for always listening to me.

Thank you for loving me no matter what I do.

Forgive me when I forsake your love.

Forgive me when I mock the ways of others.

God, please help me to understand, to always do what's right.

You are that who is, who was, who will be.

You are the living God.

You are Love.

Amen.

Kristin Ann Carl
Saint Michael School, Grand Ledge, MI

Dear God,

I go through my days feeling protected and cared for. Your infinite embrace of love is comforting. My confidence builds when I do something out of the kindness of my heart. I think of you.

Your large but gentle hands guide me through the hardships and triumphs of life. Fears vanish when I am thinking of you.

Happiness glows inside me when I have done something you would have done. When I am lost or nervous, I look to my heart and to you to gain my tranquillity. Thank you, God, for always being close to me.

Kaitlin Graham
Saint Edward the Confessor Parish, Clifton Park, NY

Guardian Angel Prayer

An angel of peace,
A faithful guide.
A guardian angel by my side.

Always protect me.
Always be near.
Watch over me
Year after year.

You are in disguise,
You are out of sight.
But I know you are there
Day and night.

Courtney Sherkel
Christ the King Parish, Houtzdale, PA

I believe in hope and dreams
    And the God that gives them.
I believe in trying to succeed
    and making the best of what I am given.
I love to read of distant lands
    for they open up new ideas to me.
They speak of gods for worshiping,
    while I say they all mean God.
As God said, "Any worship done unto another with thy whole
    heart and good intentions, I will take as worship to
    me."
I believe in unbid or unlimited faith
    for seeing isn't half of believing
    but like being blind to the greater, glorious picture.
I believe in hope that all of God's children
    will be one day safe in God's home
    and that the strife that comes with being human
    will disappear.
I believe that hope and dreams are born,
    and when I see the stars and moon
    it seems all worthwhile and I am not alone.
Amen.

Ashley Bartelt
Our Lady of the North Parish, Phillips, WI

My *heart* is to our God.
My *soul* is to our God.
My *spirit* is to our God.
For God has loved me with all his heart.

Danielle Stephanie Baca
Saint Joseph Parish, Salem, OR

Dear God

When I talk to you I feel like I can talk for hours. I know you won't tell anyone. I feel I can reveal my soul to you. I know you like it when we talk. We talk about life, love, happiness, and anything I feel I have to share.

You listen. You talk. You watch. You share with me. You love. You laugh.

We share. We love. We laugh.

You care. I care. We care.

Dear God, I know you love me, and I love you.

Amber Yokiel
Saint John the Baptist Parish, Minnesota Lake, MN

Oh, my God,

I talk to you often.

I tell you my hopes,

My dreams,

My wishes,

And my accomplishments.

I ask you for help,

For guidance,

For forgiveness.

Oh, my God,

You are the *light* of my life.

Sarah Williams
Saint Rose of Lima School, Haddon Heights, NJ

I've seen God but I can't explain it.

God is in the birds in the trees,

in the ground, in the air,

in the water,

and in you and me.

God is in everything,

So enjoy it or you'll miss everything.

Just **look.**

Jonathan Konz
Saint Adrian Parish, Adrian, MN

Dear God,
You created the earth, sea, and sky.
You created my family and I.
You created the moon, stars, and sun.
You created everyone.
You created us special in our own way.
You created us with free will to say what we say.
You knew some might turn away,
though you hoped most would stay.
You forgive those who do wrong.
You tell them you loved them all along.
To protect us from sin, you sent us your Son.
But look at what to him was done.
We didn't believe, so we crucified and killed.
But, still, with your Holy Spirit we were filled.
And in turn, we honor and worship you,
but most of all, we love you. Amen.

Rachel Obermeyer
Saint Justin the Martyr School, Saint Louis, MO

I Pray with My Fingers

The thumb, the finger nearest to me. I pray for my friends and family. They help me live life to the fullest.

The pointer finger, the finger used to teach and heal. I pray for the doctors and teachers. They use their gift of instruction and comfort for those who need it.

The middle finger, the tallest finger. I pray for the "tall" people, the leaders who direct us on our journey through life.

The ring finger, the weakest finger. I pray for the sick and the poor souls in purgatory. They need God the most.

The pinky finger, the smallest finger. I pray for myself, that I may be the best I can and live your life to meet you in heaven and eternal life.

Amen.

Stephanie Laurusonis
Saint Patrick School, Wadsworth, IL

I was thinking about you today, God.
I wondered what you look like.
And then after I thought about it,
I realized that you are beautiful.
You are the flowers and trees,
the lakes and the rivers.
You are kindness and love,
you are caring and peaceful.

You are God.

Rachel Martini
Saint Therese of the Little Flower School, Cincinnati, OH

Glory to God and prayers.
Yeah, I know all that stuff.
But somehow it hasn't real meaning,
Just saying it isn't enough.

I want a prayer that goes deeper,
A prayer that penetrates my soul.
I want a prayer to challenge,
That speaks to me as a whole.

God, hear my prayer.
And I beg you, answer my plea.
Give me a prayer with meaning,
Give me a prayer for me!

And then I begin to realize
All I had to do was believe.
With a little help from God
I trusted, and my prayer I did achieve.

Stephanie Landry
Saint Rose of Lima School, Haddon Heights, NJ

Dear God,
My love for you is greater than anything in the world. You are
the sun that brightens my day. You are the air that I breathe in
and out. You are like a friend or family member. You are the one
that understands my feelings. You are the one that helps me out
when I need it. You are the one that helps me get through the
day. You are the one that gives my family food for the table. You
are the one that will never stop loving me.

Madi Hernandez
Holy Family School, North Miami, FL

You touch me in the same way you blow every piece of grass. I may be hidden, but sooner or later I feel your mercy pour down on me like sun rays. Keep me in your sight and escort me to your kingdom.

Amy Jean Meeuwsen
Visitation of the Blessed Virgin Mary School, Forest Grove, OR

Oh, God, though we cannot see you, we know you are here.
Though we cannot touch you, we feel you at our side.
Though we cannot hear you, we listen to your wisdom.
Though we cannot smell you, we sense your divinity.
Though we cannot comprehend you, we trust you implicitly.
Though I do not know your name, I call upon you with the gift
of my faith.
Though I am but one thread in the great pattern of life, you
answer me.

I do not know what to do. Bestow upon me the blessing of
grace, your gift. Grant me the wisdom to know what
to do, the intelligence to know how to do it, and the
faith to do your will.
You gave us the world. You granted us sight and hearing to
experience it. You made every leaf green and every
flower bloom. You gave us the faith to know you, your
Son, and your work.

And we thank you, eternally satisfied.

A. R. M.
Immaculate Heart of Mary School, Atlanta, GA

As I'm lying in my bed, I pray to God, and rest my head.
As I try to recall the events of the day, all in this bed, in which I
    lay,
I realize I've done things that Christ would not do, and as the
    day went on, my sins grew, and grew.
I look out my window at a sky so starry, then, I repent, and am
    truly sorry.
Now as I lie there, and moan and groan, God forgives me
    because I'm one of his own.
Then as I look up, at the brightest star, I realize that we all are.

Cari Born
Saint Paul School, Saint Petersburg, FL

Who are you God?

Are you in the heavens and the earth?

Are you in the universe, the galaxy, and the planets in space?

Are you in the trees, the flowers, and the plants that grow?

Are you in the birds that fly and the animals that roam the earth?

Are you in the sun, the stars, and the moon that shine brightly?

Are you in the air that we breath and the water we drink?

Are you in the people who love each other?

Are you in my brothers and sisters?

Are you in the smile on children's faces?

Are you in my friends and family?

Are you in me?

Yes, I believe you are, because you are God.

Elyse Pagerly
Sacred Heart School, West Reading, PA

God,

My friend,

My shepherd,

Guide me through this day and the next. Help me to overcome the evils around me. Feed my heart and soul with all your love.

God, please forgive my sins.

Friend, lift the guilt and worries from my heart, and replace them with faith.

Shepherd, help me not to take my family, friends, life, or your love for granted.

God, thank you for the food I eat, for the pleasures I partake in, for this life itself, for my talents, for childhood so pure and true, but most of all, for every blessing you have or will ever give me.

I love and praise you, God.

Emily C.
Saint Peter Catholic Central School, Worcester, MA

Dear Jesus, Son of God, help me through this day.

On a path you lead the way, while I run and play.

When I am safe in my bed, you watch me while I lay.

Tomorrow is another day,

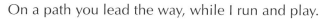

and you are with me all the way.

Amen.

Lindsey Honka
Saint Luke Parish, Shoreline, WA

Dear God,

You have loved me all my life,

every minute,

every second,

NOT ONCE have you ever stopped loving me.

Oh, God, you lift my heart,

my spirit,

my praises.

You have helped me through my hardship to happiness.

Amen.

Clarissa Matalone
Saint John Vianney Parish, Rancho Cordova, CA

Dear God,
Make your church a family that helps, forgives, and loves.
Make your church a family that you guide from up above.
Make your church a family that loves you, its sisters, and
       brothers. Make your church a family that serves you,
       and each other.
Make your church a family that works and plays side by side.
Make your church a family that no one can divide.

Austin Filippi
Saint Robert Bellarmine School, Omaha, NE

Index

Holy Rosary School
Claymont, DE
Ashley Coyle   32
Erica M. Rugis   77

Holy Spirit Parish
Indianapolis, IN
Toni Osborne   22

Holy Spirit Parish
Sioux Falls, SD
Megan Clarke   23
Pat McCann   46

Holy Trinity School
Louisville, KY
Patrick A. Bartenstein   64
Wittney Sprigg   60

Immaculate Conception Parish
Stony Point, NY
Matthew Roff   58

Immaculate Conception School
Jefferson City, MO
Dane Hughes   33
Brandi Wildhaber   14
W. J. W.   50

Immaculate Heart of Mary School
Atlanta, GA
A. R. M.   119
Name withheld   55

Incarnation School
Centerville, OH
Sarah Part   63
Colleen Suzanne Reid   68

Ladyfield Catholic School
Toledo, OH
David Fournier   90

Most Precious Blood Parish
Hazleton, PA
Lauren   32

Mount Saint Charles Academy
Woonsocket, RI
Matt Czerkowicz   29
Sarah Ramos   34

Mount Saint Joseph Academy
Buffalo, NY
Jody Allsbrook   21

Nativity of Our Lady Mission Parish
Darien, GA
Daniel Collado   88
Preston Colby Spivey   58

Nativity of Our Lord School
Orchard Park, NY
Rachel   42

Nativity School
Dubuque, IA
Mary Casey   95
Samantha Reed   24

Our Lady of Hope/Saint Luke School
Baltimore, MD
Jessica DellaRose   15
Stephanie Shindledecker   46

Our Lady of Lourdes School
Porcupine, SD
Staci Dawn Comes   54
Angel Nicole Mills   109

Our Lady of Sorrows Parish
Monroe, OH
Alex Richey   63

Our Lady of the Angels School
Columbia, PA
Crissy Hollinger   107

Our Lady of the North Parish
Phillips, WI
Ashley Bartelt   114

Our Lady of the Rosary School
Greenville, SC
Chris Carino   74
Katherine Taylor Cottle   106

Our Lady of the Sacred Heart School
Orchard Park, NY
Stephanie   86

Our Lady's Immaculate Heart Parish
Ankeny, IA
Ryan Davis   87

Owensboro Middle School
Owensboro, KY
Katie James   91

Piqua Catholic School
Piqua, OH
Logan Peltier   90

Pope John XXIII School
Middletown, OH
Megan Deaton   78

Precious Blood Parish
Trotwood, OH
Stacy Renea Mustacato   65

Queen of Peace Parish
Brodheadsville, PA
Paul Pirolli   103

Regina Elementary School
Iowa City, IA
Lauren Michael   105
Tom A. Ries   56

Sacred Heart Parish
Lacey, WA
Megan McClure   92

Sacred Heart School
Conroe, TX
Ida Clay   47
Nick Nudo   38

Sacred Heart School
Coshocton, OH
Adam Reed Fitch   32

Sacred Heart School
West Reading, PA
Lori Anne Hart   47
Elyse Pagerly   120

Saint Adrian Parish
Adrian, MN
Jonathan Konz   116

Saint Agnes Cathedral Parish
Springfield, MO
Michelle Ciesielski   12
Chinh Hoang   99

Saint Agnes School
Springfield, MO
Catherine DeSarno   61
Maggie Hediger   94

Saint Ann School
Bartlett, TN
Deanna M. Jones   11
Lindsey Tarbox   22

Saint Anne School
Houston, TX
Audrey Anne de Guzman   63
Evan L. McCarley   90

Saint Anne School
Memphis, TN
Valerie   80

Saint Antoninus School
Cincinnati, OH
Tom Gruber   93

Saint Benedict Parish
Duluth, GA
Eighth grade religious
education class   11
Special needs religious
education class   24

Saint Benedict School
Holmdel, NJ
Jaclyn   30
Conrad J. Laskowski   56

Saint Bernadette School
Brooklyn, NY
Leonard A. Billé   29
Melissa Caramico   67

Saint Bernadette School
Milwaukee, WI
Brandon J. Taylor   108

Saint Norbert School
Paoli, PA
Erin Grady   20

Saint Pascal Baylon School
Saint Paul, MN
Ashley Johnson   87

Saint Paschal Baylon School
Thousand Oaks, CA
Chelsea Wisdom   16

Saint Patrick Parish
Baton Rouge, LA
Heidi Alexandra Fontenot   12

Saint Patrick Parish
Troy, OH
Erin Ashley Grant   72

Saint Patrick School
Brighton, MI
Maddie Haigh   68–69
John M. Horal   98

Saint Patrick School
Wadsworth, IL
Stephanie Laurusonis   117

Saint Paul Parish
Oswego, NY
Colleen Furniss   38

Saint Paul School
Saint Petersburg, FL
Cari Born   120

Saint Perpetua School
Lafayette, CA
George H. Ganey   88

Saint Peter Catholic Central School
Worcester, MA
Emily C.   121

Saint Peter School
Saint Charles, MO
Shannon Hollander   79

Saint Pius X Parish
Ainsworth, NE
Carrie Lynn Anderson   51

Saint Remy Parish
Russia, OH
Dusty Francis   54
Megan Elizabeth Gariety   75

Saint Richard School
Philadelphia, PA
Michele Milano   62

Saint Robert Bellarmine School
Omaha, NE
Austin Filippi   122
Teresa Prince   21

Saint Robert School
Shorewood, WI
Emma Lueger   86
Joshua Messier   65

Saint Roman School
Milwaukee, WI
Roman Martinez   109
Amanda Wallich   36

Saint Rose of Lima School
Haddon Heights, NJ
Stephanie Landry   118
Allison Tokolish   28
Sarah Williams   115

Saint Sebastian School
Santa Paula, CA
Luis Sanchez   75

Saint Stanislaus Kostka Parish
Bay City, MI
Benjamin Adamski   48

Saint Teresa Parish
Mapleton, MN
T. R. Wede   107

Saint Theresa Parish
Oakland, ME
April Snow   57

Saint Therese of the Little Flower School
Cincinnati, OH
Erin M. Carr   66
Rachel Martini   117

Saint Therese School
Succasunna, NJ
Erin E. Esposito   85

Saint Thomas à Becket Parish
Jefferson Hills, PA
Nicole Vitale   41

Saint Thomas Aquinas School
Derry, NH
Stephanie   44

Saint Thomas Aquinas School
Wichita, KS
Brianne R. Dondlinger   76

Saint Thomas More School
Baton Rouge, LA
Arielle   92

Saint Thomas More School
Kansas City, MO
Alisan Follingstad   20

Saint Veronica School
Eastpointe, MI
Franco Fabiilli   104

Saint Vincent de Paul School
Wisconsin Rapids, WI
Caitlin Joosten   17

Saint Vivian School
Finneytown, OH
Drew Meredith Lagergren   52

Saint Wendelin School
Butler, PA
C. M.   57

Santa Barbara School
Dededo, Guam
Imee P. Fajardo   84
Hilda Marie Loria   69

Seton Catholic Middle School
Menasha, WI
Ashley M. Rachubinski   13

Villa Maria School
Erie, PA
Emily   67
Jay   97

Visitation of the Blessed Virgin Mary School
Forest Grove, OR
Amy Jean Meeuwsen   119